MW00484566

Markers:

key themes for soul survival

Mary Barton Nees

Copyright © 2017 Mary Barton Nees

All rights reserved. No part of this book may be reproduced in any form without written permission from the author.

Original Cover image by Jonny White (https://www.flickr.com/photos/velsfi/4307743390) [CC BY 2.0 (http://creativecommons.org/licenses/by/2.0)] and is licensed under the Creative Commons Attribution 2.0 Generic license.

All artwork is property of the artists cited, used by permission.

Scripture quotations, unless otherwise indicated, are taken from the New American Standard Bible® (NASB), Copyright © 1960, 1962, 1963, 1968, 1971, 1972, 1973, 1975, 1977, 1995 by The Lockman Foundation Used by permission. www.Lockman.org

Scripture quotation marked (ESV) are taken from The Holy Bible, English Standard Version® (ESV®) Copyright © 2001 by Crossway, a publishing ministry of Good News Publishers. All rights reserved. ESV® Text Edition: 2016

Scripture quotation marked (NIV) are taken from THE HOLY BIBLE, NEW INTERNATIONAL VERSION® NIV® Copyright © 1973, 1978, 1984 by International Bible Society® Used by permission. All rights reserved worldwide.

Scripture quotation marked (ERV) are taken from the HOLY BIBLE: EASY-TO-READ VERSION © 2001 by World Bible Translation Center, Inc. and used by permission.

Scripture quotation marked (ISV) are taken from the Holy Bible: International Standard Version®. Copyright © 1996-forever by The ISV Foundation. ALL RIGHTS RESERVED INTERNATIONALLY. Used by permission.

Scripture quotations marked (MSG) are taken from THE MESSAGE. Copyright © by Eugene H. Peterson 1993, 1994, 1995, 1996, 2000, 2001, 2002. Used by permission of NavPress. All rights reserved. Represented by Tyndale House Publishers, Inc.

Scripture quotation marked (TLB) are taken from the THE LIVING BIBLE copyright© 1971. Used by permission of Tyndale House Publishers, Inc., Carol Stream, Illinois 60188. All rights reserved.

ISBN: 978-1-945975-36-3

Published by EA Books Publishing a division of Living Parables of Central Florida, Inc. a 501c3 EABooksPublishing.com

To Julie, who passed the story to me, and
Anne, who helped me to dig into it.

Table of Contents

Preface

"Where does someone go to hear from God in this place?"

The bookseller stared blankly back at me.

So, I revised my question: "If I came in here troubled about 'end times'-type things, trauma, coming disasters etc. and wanted to know how to be okay with God, where would you direct me?"

The clerk led me back to a corner where I found several books about living off the grid. As he left me there I realized he must have missed *the God part* of my question. I hadn't asked him to take me to the religious book section. I didn't want someone else's commentary. I did not want a sales pitch from the personal growth section either. But even in the "prepper" section, then the New Age section, then the health section it was all looking like sales pitch to me. The number of self-help offerings reminded me of hawkers in a dizzying bazaar.

Have you walked through the bookstore lately looking for some kind of help that was better than someone else's *self*?

Have you ever wondered if the One called God were to speak or to write...and if He presumably cared to send a message into our troubled planet, what format would He use? Would He join the bazaar? Or would He hide out in a desert waiting for the hardier souls to find Him? And even if He could make sound wave echoes through time and across continents, would my ears be able to tune into His frequency?

I am going to start with a pretty safe assumption: you've already concluded that *if* He is reliable, and *if* He has really spoken, you might want to listen. Then, I'm going to lay all my cards on the table right here and say that He *has* spoken; and, what's more, He *is still* speaking.

Still with me?

My own life was turned around, and is still being changed by the words in the Bible. So I am confident that if you will expose yourself to this amazing book, you can see and hear Him for yourself. God's help is transforming way beyond the bootstrap catharsis of self-help.

We all need help! That's why self-improvement books are so popular. But even after we've read every book on the shelf, we seem to need more. God's Word is different. Unlike any other spiritual document or self-help book we might investigate[1], the Bible is the story of *how God actually enters into our world and our lives* to provide the help we need.

My seven-chapter book will ease you into most basic, repeated themes found in the ancient texts. What is called the Old and New Testaments is a remarkable collection. It is intimidating for sure, but wise, prophetic, thorough and particular, with echoes that repeat into every culture. Through story and turn-arounds (which I will explain later) you will see how some very different individuals, in very different times found their way into God's real and sustaining peace. They listened to and reckoned with the words God offers for soul survival. There's hope here if you'll take it. Think of these seven themes that I have selected as signposts to get you started into the Big Book.

I call these signposts Markers.

Introduction

The Question that Started My Own Quest

I wasn't looking for God. But the rolling train of my ambitious independence switched tracks unexpectedly at the age of 19. Wanting to climb mountains, I had snagged a job at a summer camp in Colorado. It was in Chicago's O'Hare airport where the adventure began as I linked up with an experienced hiker named Julie, who was one year younger than I. By the time we jetted to Denver, we were fast friends. Julie steered me to a Western outfitter type store and helped me select my first climbing boots. Then we headed up beyond the front range of the Rockies to her favorite spot in the whole wide world, a rustic camp for young adventurers.

Julie was vibrant and eager, like a young cat next to a moving string. She had a contagious "can do" attitude, and I was happy to be all in. We taught swimming and washed the camper's dishes, laughing and singing as we worked. In our free time, we cantered horses on open ranges. Together we trained as trail leaders, preparing to lead campers up the big climbs in the second half of the summer season. But when the Program Director posted the big trail schedule, the highest hike, Longs Peak, wasn't on the rotation next to my name.

Julie, having climbed Longs the previous summer, immediately offered to switch with me on the roster. She would take my next assignment, Apache Peak, so I could be in line for the later climb up Longs. I was thrilled at the chance to trade.

The night before she was to lead the Apache climb, we took a walk together around the camp lake. During the summer we had chattered easily about everything from the fastest way to clean up after campers to the deepest dreams we had as young women. But that night the conversation was markedly different. It was strange, really. Julie seemed uncharacteristically contemplative, wanting to broach *the spiritual*. That's the vague way I would have categorized it back then. Julie wanted to talk about God.

She could not have picked a less-invested conversation partner. I certainly wasn't interested. I personally had considered any notion of life with God a fairy tale for the weak. In fact, I had just completed a well-received paper in college on the subject. My conclusion? God was irrelevant.

But Julie remained insistent that "Abraham must have *loved* God." She was musing out loud about the ancient Hebrew Patriarch. I had heard a little of him in church going years… "Abraham must have *loved God*, Mary!" That's the way she said it. Try saying that phrase out loud with enthusiasm, and you might catch the way it lilted into my own ears.

It's interesting to me now that this phrase and her intrigue with it are the only clear details I can remember of a lengthy conversation almost 50 years ago. Her idea mixed with her genuine respect planted a longing in my soul.

I began thinking new thoughts that night: was there such a thing as really *loving* God? Was God a kind of concept that was *lovable*? Were there actually people who knew what that meant and practiced it?

The very next night I was railing at (no one else but) God. A terrible climbing accident occurred on Apache Peak the day after that pensive lake walk with Julie. For hours we waited, absorbing the description of her fall from the breathless hikers who came back without her. Then in the very early morning, a search party returned with the worst imaginable report: my friend Julie was dead. She had fallen when checking out the descent, as the campers had been packing up lunch. A loose set of rocks, a misstep, a deep slope below, and she was gone.

I was shattered. Undone. Then crying out, and later, demanding answers from those around me.

Where *was* Julie? Where had she gone?

My soul hemorrhaged with every inadequate answer others offered.

"Have faith, Mary," one friend said.

I scoffed at her. *Faith* was a religious word, which equaled to me an empty bag of air.

Another took me around the same lake for a walk, postulating, "Maybe death is like birth. It hurts and is hard, but eventually we come out to a better place."

This woman was trying to help too, but her imaginings held no weight—I recognized that much—and I returned to my bunk emptier than the mattress above me where Julie used to be.

And what about this *God* Julie had spoken so lovingly of? This silent one at whom I had been shouting? He confounded me. I was far from Him.

And that was just the beginning of journeying with Him.

In a short book like this, the treatment of such matters is meant to be a starter. My friend Julie was Jewish, and she had used a story near the beginning of the Hebrew Scriptures as the authority for her ponderings. As Julie did for me in our walk around the lake, I want to introduce you to ideas you can investigate. I have set seven signposts that can direct you on your own quest to get to know such a confounding (but very real) God.

Here, within these pages, we'll touch on key Markers from the greatest story—God's story. These archetypes keep appearing throughout His book like echoes, and they can show up in our own stories, too. Like timeless trail signs, these Markers are posted for any wanderer to see, to read, to follow. I will introduce the Marker, give you time to think on it for yourself, and then provide opportunity for further digging.

Since the prompting Julie gave me to Abraham, I've spent a lifetime pondering through the book that introduces Abraham to the world. My own introduction to that book happened not long after I got back onto campus in New York. I had put Julie's picture on the wall above my desk along with a scrap of paper where I wrote "eternal issues." I was now on some kind of quest, but I had no idea what to do or where to go with the questions on my heart. What's going on, I wondered, in all this unhappy wandering, and how does anyone know for sure anyway?

A new friend named Anne was as depressed as I was at the beginning of the term. She had experienced her own recent trauma as an exchange student. We talked of our existential questions. But soon she started coming into my room with a brand new Bible she had just started reading. This was weird. It was not what I wanted. But the strangest thing was happening (though I didn't admit this to her). The words on the pages she would find and read out loud were *electric*. Beyond being able to understand, I was experiencing the supernatural power of what Bible words can do in a hungry, thirsty soul. I spent months quietly wrestling with the implications, even as she kept coming excitedly, bravely back into my room with more.

My little book is your chance to have a friend come into the room of your heart, like Anne did with me. You can take your time with this. But if huge loss, or a fear-tinged despair is troubling you, your soul may be sending up an SOS signal. Real life can't continue while your deepest needs remain untouched. While you yet have time, now's your opportunity to take God at His word for yourself.

The Bible is full of the honest, messy struggles of people like us, who wrestled with their own big issues. This singular book, acknowledged by Jews, Christians, and Muslims, moves through many cultures, languages, and time periods, but it reads like a progressive telling from a Master who exists beyond time and then *into* cultures. It is one Big Story about us. And it is one grander story about Him. In these episodes you'll see evidence of Him, how He shapes, when He intervenes. He moves. He hangs back and waits. He speaks. He exposes. He predicts. He calls out hearts, revealing again and again that He's made a way to lead us *through* life's trauma safely back home to the very One whom Abraham learned to love.[2]

Before you too easily dismiss the Bible, at least consider what it says. Then you can make up your own mind based on some honest understanding.

My little primer and the Bible itself are not about religious answers—about one system's sales job over another. The British Anglican William Temple once said, "It's a great mistake to think that God is only or chiefly interested in religion."[3]

Religions, the opinions of men, and the ways to practice their systems don't interest me much either. Maybe you share that sentiment. However, if there really is a God, if there really is some legitimate way to hear from Him, don't you need to know?

You may not even believe in soul stuff, or any reality beyond matter and chance. My words about God speaking may seem like another empty bag of air. That's okay. I understand that position. But if you've ever stood over the grave of someone you loved, you may have already wrestled with the undeniable ache of what could come next after all we know here has ended.

These things, these soul things, matter.

Your heart is like a ticking clock, which will one day stop keeping its rhythm. You can remain independent from God, and you can own that choice. Listen to how Yeats summarized our universal problem:

Things fall apart; the center cannot hold;
Mere anarchy is loosed upon the world,
The blood dimmed tide is loosed, and
everywhere
The ceremony of innocence is drowned;
The best lack all convictions,
While the worst are full of passionate
intensity.[4]

If this is all there honestly is, then there's nothing else really to add. Close the book.

But this isn't all there is. The ceremony of innocence is drowned; yes. And some are broken and bleeding. The news shows us photos we'd rather avoid where this brokenness is all too visible. For many more, the grief and fear is locked inside. The happy help books can't touch this pain.

Perhaps you've wondered like I did: Is there more to understand than I have yet known? Is this too much to hope?

I invite you to accompany me as I lead you on the journey that took me through the pages of the Bible following the death of my friend. I will point out the markers along the trail that led me to the place of Soul Survival.

Turning and turning in the widening gyre,
The falcon cannot hear the falconer...
W.B. Yeats[5]

MARKER 1

Humility—The First Strategic Move

Where to look for this Marker: Genesis 4

The book of Genesis, that first step into the Bible's story, lays out a particular narrative of our beginning. Genesis neither denies nor sugarcoats the mess we're in as the sons and daughters of Eve.

Interestingly, the account doesn't scowl on our troubled situation either, even as earliest failure is exposed. Instead, you'll hear the simple yet weighty tale of how we got where we are and, more significantly, where hope awaits.

This opening is deep in its mythic import. But, spoiler alert: it ends badly. The 4th chapter of Genesis typifies the rest of human history as we live it. We find Adam and Eve outside the garden having just been exiled from the perfection of their beginning. Due to their own choice to go rogue on God's single watchword,[6] they must now make their own way.

That way becomes hard quickly. Chapter 4 details the first human murder—one son kills his brother—over what is the right way to worship God. Seems we've been repeating their tragedy for millennia!

Yeats, like many artists before and after him, is gloomy in his evaluation: "the blood dimmed tide is loosed" and it has been that way from near the beginning of time. Some people think that if we just get educated enough, or sophisticated enough, or kind enough (enough already) that we can end all this evil ourselves.

But I wonder if there's something *in* our bloodstream that works against every aim for peace—that which I call *soul-shalom*, or deep soul-wellness. We have some kind of memory or desire for that perfect garden, but we can't get back to it.

We don't do soul-shalom on our own very well. Every generation yearns for it, and every religious system searches for it. And though many thought we could, we haven't yet progressed past needing to find spiritual peace, whether we believe in a god or not. Human history provides just too much evidence of our profound inadequacy.

But, it's in the midst of this tragic Chapter 4, in the aftermath of that first murder, that we find a rich clue. An interesting Marker shows up in the drama that gives a word of hope about the way back to God.

Eve's Two Declarations

Eve makes a change of mind that's easy to miss but quite significant. In fact, a chasm of difference spans the consequence of the two (and only two) sentences we have from her in the post-perfect world that starts in Genesis 4. She's certainly a minor character in this chapter's narrative; the main players in the tragedy are her two sons.

But her two statements bookend the entire story, and because of their placement we can consider them a prelude and an aptly positioned epilogue from the "mother of all the living".[7]

Eve leaves us a legacy, a Marker, right in her own words:

"I have gotten..." (vs. 1)
and "God has appointed..." (vs. 25)

Simple. Yet the implications echo continually into human experience.

Look again.

In her first statement she places herself as the subject. "*I* have gotten..." She is the "getter," the one who gains, the one who attains.

What does she attain here? A son. This is a statement of accomplishment. It's also a religious statement. She adds "with the help of the Lord."[8] This is like the bumper sticker "Jesus is my co-pilot". It's as if the driver wants us to know "I've got God with me and He helps me, but I'm the one behind the wheel."

Statements like this wreak havoc. We make our declarations and then insist that God is on board with us: "*I* have gotten."

Eve is no atheist. She can't afford the luxury of such a denial—she has seen and walked with God.[9] But now she lives in a harder world, and she has to make of it what she can. She gives God some credit, but she's the leading lady. She's birthed "a manchild," she announces, and after making this initial declaration. She steps back and all hell breaks loose.

We don't hear from her again until the end of this very tragic chapter, and some time has passed. But the contrasting statement she makes at the end of her story is meant to be noticed because it's highlighted with the very same introduction: "Now the man had relations with his wife..." (vs.1, also vs. 25) and the result is another son.

However there's a striking change in sentence structure as Eve voices her subsequent birth announcement: "God has appointed me another..."

It's easy to roll on by and miss this, but look at her declaration. She has become the object of her sentence now. She has placed God in the position as head of her experience. He is now the subject of her sentence. *He* is the subject.

She knew He was around before, but now she acknowledges that He's the main actor. He's the giver. He's the appointer. Now He's the one who matters first over all her other concerns.

A Soul Pivot

This is more than just sentence structure change. True, she has spoken only words, but their arrangement tells us much about a heart shift going on. The tragedy affects all of them, but from Eve we hear these different responses, front and then back.

Her words summarize her soul life. She moves from accomplished pride to a yielded humility, and this is no minor change. We see no other actions from her. She accomplishes nothing to appease or to earn God's favor. She yields to Him, and that, fellow travelers, is pretty huge.

This is the first Marker, and it's your fork in the road.

From Genesis to Revelation you can find many other examples of this strategic turn around. The Psalms are filled with this pivoting. Eve becomes a model here, an archetype of the first real turn toward soul-shalom. She humbles herself, and she places herself back under her Creator.

Even as she lives outside Eden, Eve shows us exactly how we need to bend our souls to somehow live in connection with Him.

This is Not Religious Formula

Religions and embedded traditions have mystified anthropologists. They have gone out into the field to try to understand why humans invent such systems. Throughout time we have gone on overdrive devising our ways to try to please some concept of God. The varied visual evidence remains in the architecture and the art around the globe. From bloody appeasement rituals up step pyramids to our own "steps to success" advertisements, we continue imagining that our great aim is just around the corner. So many of these things are just strategies where we can still say *I have gotten* with a semi-satisfied smile.

Has any hint of light entered your own soul that He, your Creator, is the One in charge? That He is beyond all this strategizing? If you look into the words of the Bible, you'll find plenty of evidence of His active character. He is in the driver's seat. He knows where He's going and He has detailed the future if we care to check it out. And, He has already initiated a safe way through for us. *God has appointed.*[10]

God walks in the garden in Genesis 3. In fact, He comes looking for Adam and Eve after their failure. While they hide, He takes the initiative. He calls out for them. Think about it: the Creator Himself, who made matter actually came *into* that matter. He grounded himself to gravity, time, and space, so he could look for those whom He'd handcrafted.

And that was *after* they'd blown it.

They had strategized a way to cover their inadequacy. They had stitched together some kind of self-help with fig leaves. But it was not enough; and when God came near, they knew it.

But God came near. And He spoke.

Later, in the Psalms, in the first of a series that were sung by Hebrew pilgrims on their walk up to Jerusalem, the author exclaims: "Who is like the Lord our God, who humbles himself to behold the things that are in heaven and on the earth?"[11] "Who looks far down on the heavens and the earth!"[12]

According to these accounts, and in many other places, He's a lofty but not a despising God. He bends low, as if craning his neck toward His creation. He's a watchful, active pursuer.

One Simple Example

One afternoon I wandered into a well-stocked antique store, which had warrens of interesting rooms where I could hide. I moved slowly through, enjoying all the piles of old things beautifully arranged by someone with an artist's eye. It was not long into my reverie when I noticed a distinct hand painted sign propped by some pretty things: "Enjoy what you see, but remember, we have a working surveillance camera."

I looked up. Was there a camera somewhere? I hadn't thought of stealing, but now the thought entered my mind, and, just as quickly, got knocked out as ridiculous. Someone was apparently watching, and this began to cramp my enjoyment. I wasn't the one in charge of my pleasure now; the storeowner was. It was irritating.

Just like you, I don't like to be watched. I don't like to be judged. I would rather proceed as if the storeowner doesn't exist.

I kept musing as I slowly passed that sign. "Okay. The storeowner has a right to watch his stuff and to watch others with his stuff. I have a right to freely enjoy the stuff, under his management." My thoughts were weighing what was now in front of me.

My thought process shifted from my determination of what "I can get" for myself—to what the store owner "appointed" or arranged for me that afternoon. This was a simple but significant turn around from me as the center of activity. Not all of this belonged to me.

I amused myself with another idea: maybe right then I was being watched as I considered his pretty things. So I started a dialogue in my head "You, Mr. Surveillance Camera, can enjoy me freely looking through your stuff."

I had nothing to hide. I wasn't afraid. My way became easier. My mood certainly changed.

As I continued walking, I shifted my thinking toward God who is aware of everything happening down here, in every little hiding place as people handle His things. Can you even begin to entertain such a foreboding concept? Because I've learned some aspects of His character from reading His book, I can. He's much purer, and kinder and precisely aware than the antique storeowner with the flimsy sign.

I don't have to view God as the great cop in the sky because I can see how He reveals Himself at the very beginning and all the way through His story. He's the One who first came looking.

"Where are you?"[13] He asks because His heart leans toward us. Toward me. Toward finding each one of us out because He yearns for our restoration.

Even when we've taken stuff. Even when we've broken stuff.

At the very least, and right from the beginning, there's reason for humility from us. God Himself makes the first steps toward restoration. God makes all the first moves, and God humbles Himself to reach us. He *wants* to walk with us.

Even us. Especially us.

It took Eve some time through her own personal pain to understand this, and then she had to yield to the idea. She had lost so much already. But her own words reveal a change in her perspective. She acknowledges her soul's deep need, better met in Him.

This first fork in the road is for us. It's the narrow door.[14] You have to bend to get through, and then that bending repeats all along your way with Him. In this way, paradoxically, we start to awaken spiritually. And He starts the transformation we hadn't known we even needed. Humility before God offers the chance to consider something weighty that we hadn't cared much about before. It's our agreement to begin. The prophet Amos highlights this later in the Bible, saying that there needs be an agreement to walk between two beings.[15]

God has already agreed.

The fork in the road is yours to consider. He gave you a mind of your own, just as He did with Eve. You're individually the hold-up, here. You're the problem unless you shift your mind toward Him as the Subject of your life.

God will defer to your deliberation, and He'll wait for you to accept any appointment with Him.

This is the road less traveled. This is the narrow way. Most will go the other way, but Eve made a strategic turn here.

Stepping into that Fork in the Road

A decided change of mind about who's in charge and which way to go from here is what makes up the Eve pivot. It's an inward step. It's an awkward step. It's a strategic pivot from one's default mode of independence from God, and in some ways it feels like a seismic loss. But this pivot of heart toward God is necessary before any true journey with Him can begin. I make a simple admission that God is primary, that He is real and in charge and that it's up to me to accept His appointment.

It's that simple, yet it's wholly significant.

Results Come in Time

Eve's shift of soul starts a multiplied reaction that remains evident in the generations that come from her third son, named Seth. Later on from the line of Seth, we learn of Enoch, his 7th direct descendant. Enoch is the first man mentioned in the Bible as one who *walked with God*.

Wait—in the earliest record of biblical characters, didn't everyone sort of walk with God?

Nope. Walking with God was a distinguishing mark even early on.

According to God's record, the people who actually walk with Him are rare.[16] God places a huge value on our choices, and He has taken great risk in giving us that choice. And boy, have I struggled with that.

Why would He risk letting us make such huge messes in every generation? Why doesn't He "do a better job" of controlling us? He seems willing to allow abuse of His own reputation, not to mention the tragic fallout in history, for the sake of giving us such costly freedom.

Most people, then and now, choose to go their own way with abandon. But Scripture highlights, commends, and rewards one man for going against the tide: Enoch, descendant of Seth. He actually "walked *with* God."

Eve's heart shift in Genesis 4—her pivotal soul shift—set the pattern for Enoch, who came after her. Like Eve, Enoch humbled himself. He stepped back onto the path, under the authority and into the reality of where God was walking.

Consider the Pivotal Marker

If your soul is desperately troubled, if there's an ache inside that others haven't been able to touch, I want to encourage you. You're potentially in a strategic place.

There's a fork in the path. There's a Marker here for you.

This is a necessary beginning for your soul's true adventure. Take courage—others have gone before you and left this humble Marker as a sign. Look to the God who's looking for you.

Humble your independent soul. God made it and handcrafted it to find its soul-shalom first and finally in Him. Allow Him to oversee it.

Echoes of this MARKER: Humility

1. Find a Bible and look into the lives of any one of these men and women to see if you can identify an "Eve Pivot". Keep in mind that for God-followers, this pivot is not always at the beginning of their particular story. Then often, such yielding reappears. Here's just a sampling.

   - Abraham: Genesis 15:1-7

   - Leah: Genesis 29:21-35

   - Joshua: Joshua 5:2-15

   - David then Abigail: 1 Samuel 24:1-15, 1 Samuel 25:1-38

   - Lamentations (of Jeremiah) 3:1-28

   - Centurion: New Testament, Matthew 8:1-10

   - Stephen: New Testament, Acts 6:8-7:60

2. Can you name a time or an experience when you knew that you would not be safe if you were the one in charge of your own life?

3. If this is true, what do you need to do?

Alice by Aaron Gosser

If I could wish for something it would be
neither wealth nor power,
but the passion of possibility.
Soren Kierkegaard[17]

MARKER 2

Prayer—Then Begins the Dialogue

Where to look for this Marker: Exodus 3:1-4, Exodus 33:11, Psalm 90

My grandfather called prayer "wishful thinking," and he took pride in this dismissal. My other grandfather said nothing about prayer, but I clearly remember how he would "say grace" before the Thanksgiving meal. He lowered his head and spoke personally, as if someone other than those sitting at the table was actually listening. I remember peeking up to watch as he prayed, curious that he seemed to really think he was talking to God.

It was merely one moment at one meal, but I still can feel the wonder of it. I didn't know a whole lot else about prayer until later when I grew desperate.

What exactly is this simple thing we call prayer, and how did it first begin in God's story?

Prayer's Beginning

Genesis lets us in on Eve's pivot and then the focus shifts to her third son, Seth: "Then men began to call upon the name of the Lord."[18] This very last sentence in that tragic narrative of Genesis 4 gives us more to appreciate after Eve's choice to humble herself under God.

Cain killed Abel, Eve's second son. Nothing would reverse that for Eve or her family. Cain was banned and locked in his own struggle, but Eve, and then Seth after her, give us an indication of the way through human trauma. After her pivot: "*then* men began to call upon the Lord."[19] Look at the progression as the story lays it out:

1. She humbles herself
2. Prayer begins

Prayer is simply what this passage says—calling on God. Now, on a basic level, that's not difficult. Prayer is no more complicated than that in its purest form.

Prayer, then, is doable.

But prayer is also a learning process, for (wonder of wonders) we're engaging in conversation with a listening God. Prayer can mature. That potential deepens after the first "calling upon."

I love how the Bible later describes prayer in Moses' story: "The Lord would speak to Moses face to face, as a man speaks with his friend."[20] Prayer has potential to be an honest and intimate dialogue like one has with the best of friends.

But think about it—the conversations you had with a best friend didn't happen your first meeting. What did it take for you and that friend to build to such a relationship?

Moses' Learning Curve

According to the Torah (the first 5 books of the Bible), Moses wasn't born knowing how to pray. Prayer is a practice he had to learn—in other words, he didn't just pick up where Eve's third son, Seth left off. Like all of us, Moses had to start from scratch.

In fact, the Hebrew record places Moses in the wilderness, rejected and displaced at an old age, when his learning curve with God begins. His story is similar to the beginning we saw in the opening of Genesis: Moses, like Adam, isn't looking for God when God comes searching for him.

This is how prayer began for Moses: something out of the ordinary caught his attention and he stopped to ponder it. Something unusual happened.

That's it.

The text in Exodus 3 says that Moses *turned aside*. He literally spoke to himself—he deliberated, and then he decided to try to figure out what he was seeing.

There, in his path, was a desert bush aflame, "burning...yet not consumed."[21]

God was in that bush. Moses certainly didn't know that, but he decided to explore the strange thing happening right in front of him. The text highlights that Moses' choice here, like Eve's before him, bore spiritual consequences.

When the Lord saw "that he turned aside to look," God called to him from the midst of the bush, "Moses, Moses!" And Moses responded, "Here I am."[22]

The dialogue has begun. Like a richly-toned Black American spiritual—first a call and then a response—together voices form the meter of the song.

This is when things ignite spiritually for Moses. He had tried earlier in his life to direct God's work and failed.[23] But now God comes in. He takes initiative at a particular time, and Moses responds.

It's safe to say that Moses wasn't on a spiritual quest that day. Even so, he stops and ponders. God notes Moses' decision to turn aside, speaks to him, and initiates what will be a long relationship.

Examples of Growing Intimacy

Moses has a lot to learn, but he does learn, and that's what's so encouraging. Here's a fragment of one of his later prayers:

"For a thousand years under Your sight are like yesterday when it passes by, or like a watch in the night...so teach us to number our days so we may present to You a heart of wisdom," he pleads with God in Psalm 90.[24]

Moses' story shows us it is possible to learn spiritually, to learn of God intimately, to have face-to-face interaction with Him. You can hear Moses' longing for others to catch on to this in the rest of Psalm 90. Moses' story illustrates how we begin with an 'Eve Pivot' somewhere along our path, humble ourselves, and then call to God in prayer.

It's possible to learn to pray to Him, to learn to love Him like a friend. Some do. Many do not.

Moses did. Before him, Abraham did.

Jesus did too. The Gospels reveal Jesus' intimacy with the One he called his Father. As a faithful Jew, Jesus would have learned the texts of his ancestors starting at an early age.[25] We get a glimpse of this in Luke's account, which shows that the boy Jesus was remarkable as a listener and learner of spiritual things.[26]

Then, when he goes missing one day on the way home from one of the holy feasts, his mother and father find Jesus "in my Father's house" back in the temple of Jerusalem. Referring to the Creator as "Father" was not completely unheard of in Judaism,[27] but the personal and literal intimacy that Jesus expressed was rare and likely shocking. After all, Jews are careful and respectful when and how they pronounce or even write G-d's name. Here, Jesus calls Jehovah his *Dad*.

Was this brash? Apparently not. The text immediately adds that Jesus "continued to grow in wisdom and stature. God was pleased with him and so were the people who knew him."[28] Jesus' spiritual life developed quietly, behind-the-scenes, as he grew. He established a relationship with God as Father or 'Abba.'

When Jesus becomes a man and initiates his public work, we learn of his prayer life through the observations and written record of his followers. In Jesus' first sermon, detailed by Matthew, he contrasts between religious practitioners who make a public display of their prayers "to be noticed"[29] "in order to be seen by men"[30] and those who pray "in secret," in a place where they alone are actually conversing with the One they are trusting.

Jesus continues that it's not about the words (how many or how fervent)—it's about trusting that God is really there, that He's a good Father who hears, and that He will speak.

I unconsciously did that in the antique store after I saw the manager's sign. I admit I first started a dead-end imagination with "Mr. Surveillance Man," but Surveillance Man cannot know, let alone respond to my thoughts. God can and does. He's very good with me.

While it has taken some time to grow in this relationship, God planted the possibility of prayer like a seed within me long before.

How Prayer Started for Me

As a child I heard a verse from the Bible that caught me. Jesus gives an open invitation "to ask...to seek...and to knock." He doesn't just invite the seeker—he gives an audacious triple-guarantee that "everyone who asks receives, and he who seeks finds, and to him who knocks it shall be opened."[31]

Jesus went on to emphasize that "your Father in Heaven" will respond better than we do. "You're at least decent with your own children. So don't you think the God who conceived you in love would be even better?"[32]

I remember wondering, could that be true for me?

But I forgot that question as my years advanced. Dismissing God was easy.

What I didn't know was that these words of promise from Jesus waited silently in my memory. And when I was mourning Julie's death, an idea came at me 'out of the blue.' "Maybe I could count on God, according to what He once said (ask...seek...knock) to help me find answers."

Now as I read Moses' account at the bush, it all seems familiar to me. Moses got a fiery bush; I had a silent, long-forgotten promise in my head. Both of these encounters came by surprise. Both were arresting. Both took some deliberation. For me, the words of Jesus sprang to life. I agreed to investigate.

You Learn It by Doing It

Jesus didn't just talk about prayer; he practiced it, wordlessly and sometimes openly. The disciples observed this. One follower of Jesus finally came to him and asked for some instruction in prayer. He saw Jesus doing it, then this man realized he needed it too. Jesus offered help simply because he was asked.[33] Then his followers started to learn to pray.

Jesus' prayer life became a catalyst for much more prayer. And these prayers have multiplied through the centuries ever since he uttered his last prayers in agony from a wooden Roman cross.

The simplest takeaway from the examples of Moses' and Jesus' lives is that prayer is a learned personal practice. Prayer is a "talking with God" dialogue that has a beginning point. It can then develop into an even more mature rhythm of communication. I'm calling it communication because there really is someone on the other end of the line.

A Hebrew pilgrim declared it this way: "I love the Lord, because he hears."[34] Oh, the beauty in that simple statement. I say it now also with such gratitude. Whoever first voiced that had learned its validity by doing it.

Prayer begins as a private expression of trust in God. It grows because God reinforces and rewards it. What's more, He answers your first calls and replies to your responses. It's a dialogue.

When you look at mature examples, as we have with both Moses and with Jesus, it may seem like you'll never get there. But remember, as with Seth at the end of Genesis 4, prayer begins by simply "calling on God."[35]

Prayer is a Marker

If prayer is a Marker, then it's one that moves with you after the fork of humility. Prayer can be likened to the trail blaze signs visible all along your journey. The trekker looks up regularly, notes the presence of the Marker, is silently reassured and directed.

But maybe that's a pale comparison. We're talking about communion with a living being called God. *He* goes along with us. We can walk and talk with Him. This, truly practiced, is a radical hope, yours for the asking.

What will it take for you to begin?

Echoes of this MARKER: Prayer

1. What was prayer in your earliest experience?

2. Read the story of any one of these individuals, excerpted below, and list what you learn about the circumstances that prompt prayer. Then identify specifically what they ask and how they ask.

   - Abraham: Genesis 18:16-33

   - Moses: Exodus 33:1-23

   - Hannah: 1 Samuel 1:1-20

   - Daniel: Daniel 9:1-22

   - Nehemiah: Nehemiah chapter 1 through to 2:5

   - Jesus: New Testament: Luke 22:32-46

   - Prayer meeting: New Testament: Acts 12:1-16

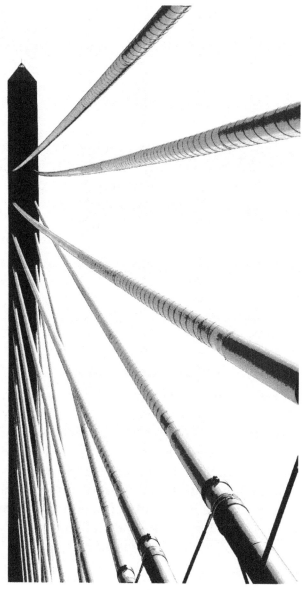

Cable Connection by Diane S. Hirt

I think that everything which is really good
and beautiful—of inner moral, spiritual and
sublime beauty in men and their works—
comes from God.[36]
Vincent Van Gogh

But, wretched as we are, and more so than if
there were no greatness in our condition, we
have an idea of happiness, and cannot reach
it. We perceive an image of truth and possess
only a lie. Incapable of absolute ignorance and
of certain knowledge, we have thus been
manifestly in a degree of perfection from which
we have unhappily fallen.[37]
Blaise Pascal

MARKER 3

Fear and Grace—One is Not Complete Without the Other

Where to look for this Marker: Genesis 4:17-24 and Genesis 6:5-8

Eve made a strategic pivot. Moses made that pivot, then learned to pray. For both, this marked the beginning of a long and difficult path. God predicted that Eve's life would be hard.[38] We can read chapters about Moses' excruciating trial of leadership.[39]

Is this typical? Are all earnest walks with God hard?

I believe our default nature is darker than we can grasp, and human history confirms this. The Bible makes this plain in the story of every God-follower.

Many books on spiritual journey will avoid confronting this difficulty. That's why I call them "sales pitch". Because it won't take you long in any Bible reading to see that God has a standard for right called Holiness, and His perfection is beyond our reach. To dismiss this is maybe "nicer" but it is not honest. It's important to grapple with God's supreme "otherness", because even when you pivot in humility before Him, you're still going uphill and the grade often gets steep.

Does this mean the bar with Him is too high? Why even start? When I was considering God, standing at the fork in my own path, the whole idea of trying to live a life "rightly" on what I assumed would be His way was a huge turn-off. The last thing I wanted was some kind of religious treadmill.

Humility I "got." Actually, my experience with Julie's death constrained me to face facts with some humility (making a pivot even as I re-word this). Then I began to get comfortable with prayer. But living right? How does one even do that?

This next Marker in God's story demonstrates how any human makes it through in any walk with God.

Through-Hikers

We live near the Appalachian Trail. We love to show visitors a bit of the historic pathway that cuts through the entire mountain range from Georgia up to Maine.

But as we take day hikes we sometimes encounter what are called "through-hikers."

These guys are unmistakable because they're a mess. That's the first thing you'll catch from far off. They also walk with more purpose than day-hikers. They have more gear for the long haul, and their equipment looks carefully selected and well-used.

Let's go back to the idea introduced in an early chapter of Genesis, mentioned simply as "walking with God".[40] If your travel partner is the Creator, how do you realistically keep up on such a journey? What kind of equipment should you bring? What kind of expectations should you have?

The idea is crazy to me, for God is, by definition, perfect. What if I stink too much? What if I neglect the way He traverses a log and I trip? What if I just get sick of this whole thing and want to quit? How will He feel about me then?

God's view of me may not have been my first concern, but if He exists, His view remains the ultimate verdict on my life. This is not a day hike with Him. And facing any idea of His present reality, I soon realize that I'm in peril if I assume I can ever adequately perform with or alongside One who is Holy. In desperate situations your soul may be already wrestling with this. But for the most part, we all do a really crafty job of ignoring any thought of dealing with God.

But Things Fall Apart

Did you ever notice that a thing left to itself always decays? A spinning top set in motion will eventually peter out. All organic things move from structure to randomness. A cup of hot or icy water will move toward the ambient temperature around it until its energy is no different than the degree of its surroundings. There's a natural law that actually names this: it's called entropy.[41]

I remember when I learned this in a physics class. I found relief, actually, because the law called out what already troubled me. Science can't answer why, but natural things don't have the capacity to sustain their own vitality. Organic bodies just don't last—not a single one of them.

Something from outside the system needs to re-energize natural things. Every organism is decaying. We're all moving away from perfection, from our original state.

Okay. So if everything decays, how is any spiritual vitality even possible? Are we dreaming? Where's the trail Marker here? I need some help.

The next examples from the Bible give us much to consider about finding real peace with God when things go south. The mode for so many of us, as in the beginning, is that we typically care *little* about God and what He's said until things get hard. "The store manager and his stupid surveillance camera be damned." This is a normal attitude toward authority—at least it's been mine.

As things get darker, mockers get bolder, bad behavior multiplies. Entropy—or breakdown—increases.

There's nothing new here. It's all happened before. The Bible lays it out.

Facing the Problem

In Genesis 4, contemporaneous with Eve's turning to God in humility, one of her relatives makes a brash claim.[42] This man, Lamech, is the 7th generation from Adam through their first son, the murderous Cain. Lamech boasts proudly that he too is a murderer, possibly a double murderer. He declares to his double wives that he merits a multiplied reproach from God (whom he mocks in disbelief).

He has no fear.

He has no regard for God, yet his scoffing (likely made in what he thought was the privacy of his own surroundings) got recorded. God didn't miss it. And for us, Lamech's example is written down.

The decay is multiplying.

But God always gets the last word on everything we say and do, even privately. God may give this time; He may give us *lots* of time. In the end, however, evil's effects come to the light, and all mockery ends. To really face this honestly brings fear. But there's something else that comes along with this sense of foreboding.

Evidence of Ancient Through-Hikers

Shortly after Lamech's boast we find the genealogy of Seth's generations. The 7th from Adam's line through Seth is Enoch who proves to be wholly different than his parallel, boasting cousin. The contrast between them is intentional. Enoch, you will find, is one who first "walked with God".

Genesis doesn't explain how Enoch does this amazing thing. Instead it narrates this simple fact and states it twice.[43] Rabbis have said that if something is worth saying, it is emphasized twice. For one to walk with God given the downstream pull of entropy is an achievement of considerable note, especially when people like Lamech are around.

Lamech boasts. Enoch keeps on walking. God is very aware of both of them.[44]

Enoch, Noah, then enters the Fear of God

This Enoch, descendant of Seth—Eve's third son, is the one who "began to call upon God".[45] Enoch, then, comes from that line after Eve's strategic pivot.[46] Enoch goes further than Eve or Seth did, for it is of him that we first hear the concept of "walking with God." How did Enoch learn this in such difficult times, and how did this through-hiker keep going?

There's nothing in his description that gives us any clue, but we do get substantial information about Enoch's great-grandson, Noah. He too was one of those rare ones who "walked with God"—the Hebrew account gives us that same unique phrase describing him.[47]

The years are even darker by the time Noah is walking. Decay has further multiplied, and according to the recounting of this early history,[48] we hear God's view on this.

> The Lord saw how great the wickedness of the human race had become on the earth, and that every inclination of the thoughts of the human heart was only evil all the time. The Lord regretted that he had made human beings on the earth, and his heart was deeply troubled. So the Lord said, "I will wipe from the face of the earth the human race I have created—and with them the animals, the birds and the creatures that move along the ground—for I regret that I have made them.[49]

Take Him at His word and you'll feel something called fear. "The Lord saw...his heart was deeply troubled...I will wipe..."

God has made a determination of judgment. He announces His intent before He acts.[50] He tells us exactly what He sees and what He knows about the private thoughts of men. He also reveals the private emotions of His own heart, "filled with pain."

In this account, God's verdict hangs over Noah and all those of his time like a guillotine hovering over humanity's collective neck. And God's opinion (and His ability to act on what He states) stands as absolute. The rest of this story gives us that account.

God, whom Jesus called "Father," not only has the ultimate right but also the responsibility to say when enough is enough. Despite what the Lamechs of the world may dismiss in denial, the Creator of all things gets to decide. God is the Judge, and true judgment has to do with pure justice, something we all yearn for (when it comes to what others do) yet cower under, or mock (when it comes to our own lives).

When Fear Becomes Necessary

Fear is the next Marker. We've had a fork in the road, we have trail blazes and a sense of God's communication along the way now. Fear is the big warning sign at the edge of a cliff. It startles us; we can't miss it. We need this fear in order to remain safe. This Marker, heeded, directs behavior. Noah, for example, gets pretty busy after hearing this warning from God.

Fear proved necessary for many in the Bible. Abraham, the Hebrew patriarch Julie had spoken of, once blurted out as he encountered a wicked town, "there is no fear of God in this place."[51] According to the Patriarch the only thing worse than fear is *no* fear. Abraham feared when he said this, because he'd also learned from experience that fearing *God* was the only way to safety in trauma.[52]

Abraham deals with God in prayer[53], and God resolves Abraham's dilemma. Fearing God trumps all other fears then, because it can direct us right into God's path of rescue.

Fear Introduces Grace

Fearing God is a strange thing to understand, especially in our time where it's so easy to live a life insulated from God. But biblical fear is a transcendent, troubling ache, a sort of sullen dread that can't be shaken. The wise king Solomon said later in the Bible that such fear is the *beginning*...[54] In God's story and in all His dealings with people, fear sets the stage for hope and grace to follow.

Immediately after God states the judgment hanging over Noah's world, the Scriptures provide a prophetic declaration of surprising hope: "But Noah found favor in the eyes of the Lord." (Genesis 6:8)

Stop and take in that sentence. The context is desperate. God had just pronounced worldwide destruction. It's as if my antique storeowner has announced that he's about to bulldoze his looted shop. But then comes this bullhorn announcement of rescue for one who remains in the store. The sentence is a deliberate contrast between fear and fear's way out.

"But Noah..."

Genesis 6 tells the story amidst multiplied chaos. God also details the chaos as "wickedness", "violence", and "evil." He names it. He tells us how He feels about it and what He's going to do.

But Noah.

The language places this as a deliberate signal of the heart of God toward rescue. When fear is attended to as a Marker, a complimentary but very different Marker shows up right behind it.

"But Noah found favor in the eyes of the Lord."

The Beginning of Grace

Look at these words more closely: Noah "found" favor. God's favor had to be discovered, and discovery suggests searching.

Noah's "favor"—the first use of the vital biblical concept often translated as *grace*—is another quiet but extremely significant archetype that shows up in the Bible again and again.[55]

Note that grace is bestowed upon Noah, not manufactured from inside of him. Does

Noah drum up his rescue by his own excellence and submit it as a bargaining chip before God?

No. God takes the initiative here, and the text is clear on this: grace comes "in the eyes of the Lord." In fact, many times when "grace" is used in the Bible it is coupled with this phrase *in the eyes of the Lord.* It seems, by the language, that it's important to understand the source of this thing we'd like to have.

Looking into Him

The day my insides soured in the antique store, reckoning again with God righted me. It's *in Him*, not in me or anyone else that grace originates. I can't "get grace" any more than Eve could get a manchild on her own. I can't take credit for it. I can't make it happen.

It's an appointed thing that comes from God, a gift sourced from His heart into mine. Humility, prayer, fear, then grace.

We speak of grace so casually. We appreciate receiving nice things we didn't expect. But the function of biblical grace highlights our need and God's provision for desperate rescue. Fear stops us, *then* grace can gather us.

The value of fear is that it focuses us. Fear has the potential to direct our search for God. That's what happens with Noah, later with Abraham, and later still with so many others.

To look into God is a fearful thing. Face just that idea and you'll be on to something. Failure keeps us hiding from Him. Noah has courage. He's already been walking with God, but he explores further. The sustaining grace that Noah receives from God is transforming. It's his *only* hope for rescue.

"But Noah found grace in the eyes of the Lord."[56]

How did he do this? God says later to Moses: "no man can see me and live."[57] That's the frightening reality from God's mouth. So, how could it be possible for Noah to have any legitimate expectation of such favor? Being "face to face" with God is a stance of intimacy. The phrase "in the eyes of the Lord" is a personification we can understand. God is spirit, not limited to time and space, but the idea that God has eyes with which He can see, that He knows every intent of our hearts, that He decides and has deep emotion, that He can be faced, could not be plainer in these narratives.

Noah faced that fear, somehow looked into God, and was given grace. Many years later, Moses discovers the same God.

Jesus' View of Your Need

Jesus was direct about this. True spiritual life travels only in one direction: *from* God into us. We may produce our own fireworks for a few moments, but they always die out. What ignites us spiritually and eternally has to come from outside our system.

Jesus' view of human ability on its own apart from God was bleak and candid: "For I say to you that unless your righteousness surpasses that of the scribes and Pharisees, you shall not enter the kingdom of heaven."[58]

There's no hope at all in that statement.

Jesus said that righteousness won't come from us. We can't manufacture it. In fact he said that what comes out from us is "defiled."[59]

He explained this further with a metaphor: "the lamp of the body is the eye."

Your whole body is lit through the agency of your eyes being trained on the original flame: God Himself. Apart from that light source, which must come into the dark cavities of your body and your soul, you exist in abject spiritual lost-ness, and *"how great is the darkness!"*[60]

Think about this physiologically: there's no light inside your body cavity. That's a physical fact. When scopes go in they must bring their own light with them. With the added light, the physician can see; without it, the scope only registers complete blackness.

Your eyes, which Jesus said were lamps, are designed with receptors—receiving lenses that gather light then transmit it to your brain, enabling you to see. The light must come in however for your receptors to work.

You're like the moon: it has no inherent light of its own. Rather it reflects the light that shines onto it. God is like the sun.

You, therefore, are only a receiver of light and love and goodness. According to Jesus, you simply can't generate these powers on your own.

Religious people and the self-improvement crowd don't like to hear this. They imagine that they can "do something" of merit all by themselves. But spiritually-needy people already know their poverty.

Where Righteousness Comes From

What the Bible tells us from front to back is that we're in trouble, but we also see repeated evidence for God's way of rescue.

"Blessed are those," said Jesus, "who hunger and thirst for righteousness, for they shall be satisfied."[61]

There's the hope he's offering right there. We must desire, "hunger and thirst" for this quality of righteousness, and then it comes to us gift-wrapped. Fear. Then grace.

We're given what we need to know. Somehow Noah's eyes fixed on God. That's enough. We find our rescue by looking into God ourselves. And for Noah, this is the turning point that rescues him and his household. Grace from God, His way, in His time, is the only way out.

Moses, too, turns to consider that strange, fearsome thing—the bush in the desert that burned but wasn't consumed. He stopped to evaluate and met the source of the light, God Himself.

Moses calls Him "He who was in the bush."[62] I love that personal statement of his. Moses learned to know the transcendent One who dwelled *in* that strangely-lit bush. Meeting Him changed everything for Moses that particular day and sustained him all the way through his journey until the end.

For me, the beginning was "He who was on the walk." After Julie died I'd determined to find the real truth about this God who could take away life. I knew I could at least find God because of that seed of hope from Jesus that I had picked up as a young child—about asking, seeking and knocking. Somehow I trusted that encouragement.

Even so, I stumbled around for months in my search. I resisted religious answers, but words in the Bible penetrated my defenses poignantly and personally. I was being treated to grace.

Enough for the Road Ahead

These examples from Noah, Abraham, and Moses are meant to be instructive. God is findable, and when found, He ignites and sustains. He satisfies and rescues. He reverses entropy! He knows who I am, who you are, and what we're doing. He has eyes. That's an intimidating reality—in context it's even more intimidating because danger is coming.

He *sees*.[63]

He knows the future and He feels deeply about it. He evaluates it all, and He will act. Judgment hangs heavy and ready. Without His grace, we're completely lost, but in God's eyes—intimidating though his eyes are—we find spiritual rescue.

The old song *Amazing Grace* captures the sequence of how this grace is found: "T'was grace that taught my heart to *fear*...and grace my fears *relieved*."

Suspended judgment from God hangs overhead but intervention is still possible, still available in God. Grace is His character; it comes out of His eyes. We can't meet what's ahead of us alone. Whoever remains on their own will be lost in their own inadequacy.

We already saw in Genesis chapter 6 that apart from this grace, God's judgment upon the earth would have included Noah and his family as well. How did Moses, how did Enoch, how did Noah sustain their soul lives? There's only one source of soul life.

You find it only by looking into Him.

Echoes of these MARKERS: Fear then Grace

1. In any of these accounts, locate the point of Fear. Then linger there to gain understanding. What do you think is the root problem causing such fear? Next look for any sure sign that Grace is given in the wake of that fear.

   - Adam and Eve: Genesis 3:1-24

   - Hagar: Genesis 21:9-21

   - Joseph: Genesis 50:15-21

   - Rahab: Joshua 2:1-21

   - David: 2 Samuel 12:1-15, also Psalm 51

   - Paul: Romans 7:6 through to 8:4

   - John: Revelation 1:3-19

2. From what you've seen so far, how would you describe Grace?

Night Soundings by Mary Nees

Markers

There is only one thing I fear in my life, my
friend. One day the dark will swallow the red.
Mark Rothko[64]

MARKER 4

Prophecy—Your Trail Map

*Where to look for this Marker: Genesis 2:16-17
and Genesis 3:1-19*

Mark Rothko, an important abstract colorist in 20th century America, saw his own future. In any culture, in every time, artists seem to sense important things ahead that they can hardly understand.[65]

Rothko was gifted with a provocative sense of vision. He could see what was coming, but he had no power to live with his vision. Tragically, his body was found on the floor of his studio some twelve years after uttering the quote on the previous page with his wrists slit and his body infused with anti-depressants.

It's not the worst of despair that can ruin you unless all you see ahead is despair. We're all so vulnerable. Even the strongest and most mature among us can be emotionally undone very quickly. If you knew your own future, would it make a difference as to how you live now?

For Mark Rothko, the future he feared came to be.

The Bible answers our need for a reliable view on what's ahead. The next Marker, the words concerning the future given by the biblical prophets, is like a trail map that is glimpsed in portions throughout the whole Bible. For any journey with God, you'll need to understand this Marker.

Hope For The Long Haul

One week not long ago we dialogued with an honorable man who has been falsely convicted and will go to prison. That same week, I connected with a young physician who gave her life to serve the poor in Nepal but is now stuck taking chemo drugs in a hospital in Chicago. Then I prayed for a mom I know who was planning the funeral for her teenage daughter.

All of these friends have sat alone in early morning darkness looking despair in the face. All of them found their wrestling spirits strengthened by the big-picture words of promise encased in God's book: that view He gives in His book that reveals what is coming beyond the despair. Each of these strugglers chose to get in God's face to make sure they had His view right.

One November, while turkey cooked, the Thanksgiving parade flickered on the TV screen. I looked up and noticed on the Macy's department store edifice, positioned right where cameras would capture it at every act, a big bright sign: "BELIEVE." That word sounds hopeful, I suppose, cheerful, quasi-religious—whatever. People toss that word BELIEVE around like it's a magic energy pill.

I thought then of my friends mentioned above and wondered, what are they supposed to do with an advertisement like that? Believe what? I'm not sure the Macy's BELIEVE would've helped Mark Rothko much either if he had lived to consider it.

When Julie died and desperation plagued me, the words "have faith" meant so little. If the person who said that to me meant "try hard to just believe" then I was hopeless. I found little in that nice word to give me any surety. It sounded to me like a ladder propped up against nothing.

Belief all by itself is meaningless. It's like the helium that inflates the parade balloons—it might look impressive for a little while, but soon it loses its lifting power. For the act of believing to have any merit it must be tied to something solid, something worth believing. Faith takes on meaning only when it has a reliable object. This really helped me once I understood that the focus is not *my* ability to conjure up BELIEF, but rather *His* TRUSTWORTHINESS.

For example: the chair I sit in when I type is well-constructed and time-tested. I don't debate whether or not it'll hold me when I sit down. I had faith this morning that it would do again what it has shown it does well: hold my weight. I didn't have to think about this; I simply believed what I already knew was true about the chair.

There's nothing impressive about that; the chair is the point, not my believing in it. To sit down on something I only imagined in my head would have led to a fall. Therefore, the chair is the reliable object, not my faith. And my faith in my chair means nothing unless I literally connect with the chair.

The chair that can hold you up in life is the reliability of God's character. It is seen in the words He has given us. These words reveal Him—they build our confidence. *He* must be the object of our faith. Belief on its own or in anything else will be wholly disappointing. It will fail when it is tested. What's more, God's book gives hope because He shows His plan throughout His words.

My struggling friends know what they've already experienced with God in their past; and though the present is very bleak, they are trusting what He's said about their futures. In each case their believing is not the point.

What they believe *in* is the point; and His words are their only solace against real and current odds.

Those who know these folks are privileged to witness the evidence of their conviction. There's a glimmer of light in their weary eyes. In each case they're looking beyond their present trauma into the promises of a God who can be trusted.

This kind of trust, directed right at Him, has the power to sustain. *God has stated* this and demonstrated it in many places in His book. Beyond revealing His heart, He has given many detailed glimpses into a future only He could know, only He has the authority to guarantee.

He has a plan. He is carrying it out.

To various prophets God dictated specifics with complete reliability.[66] He's given us a detailed trail map.

The Purpose of Prophecy

Here's a bird's-eye view of all the biblical statements about the future: both the Old and New Testaments end with significant prophetic portions. If read as a trail map, the Bible prepares us for what's coming. In fact, approximately 25% of all scriptures, when written, were words speaking definitively of things to come.[67] That's one in every four verses.

Parents get tired of hearing "Are we there yet?" But God doesn't. Parents try to be creative with ways to help children mark and imagine time, distance, and eventuality.

I remember making a chain of construction paper loops so our little ones could better understand the waiting days before Christmas. Each day, excitedly another loop got torn off as we got closer and closer. At least with the loops they had a visual to handle time's slow movement.

God, our Father, anticipates our inability to grasp what's coming and when. He has provided imagery, with variety, and with much communication to aid our limited view. Prophecy is one of the distinctives that sets the Bible apart from any other spiritual literature.[68] God knows what's ahead and He speaks about it (a lot) in the Bible. No man-made book would risk such unproven disclosure.

Two Basic Categories of Prophecy

For the sake of simplification, the broad collection of biblical prophecies can be grouped into two main categories:

1. Warnings with a coming result
2. Unconditional promises for the future

Some of these prophetic statements point to a specific person, such as the prophet Elisha's strange prediction for healing from leprosy[69] or King Hezekiah's grant from God for fifteen added years to his life.[70]

Both were simple promises, and many individual interventions like these exist; but the bulk of prophecies are multi-layered in their application to many people throughout time. Words about the future fit into two categories: warnings and promises. And sometimes warnings and promises are wrapped up together.

These writings resemble ripples in a pool with waves of fulfillment. Of course, because sometimes the writing can be symbolic and a good portion of it is yet to be completely fulfilled, the dissecting can be tricky. But let's look at the basics in this overview.

God uttered to Adam the first prophecy in human history. This is the first type of prediction, a warning:

"But you must not eat from the tree of the knowledge of good and evil, *for when you eat of it you will surely die.*"[71]

This was a sure projection into the future. God directed this word to Adam, but it also applied to Eve and through them to all of mankind. I've often thought that Adam and then Eve could not have had any experiential clue as to what God meant when he voiced "you will surely die." They didn't know death.

And even if God did explain the idea to them further, after Eve took the bite, I imagine her checking her pulse and thinking, "hmmm...guess I'm good. Nothing's happened."

But what God predicts is always true, always reliable. The time lag between God's statement of this eventuality and her experiencing it was an extension of mercy. That it took time doesn't mean it wasn't true. God gave her time to ponder before her death. Time was her opportunity for reflection.

Time is a gift. God gives us time to consider and turn to Him.

The death that He predicted, the entropy that started that very moment they ate and which eventually placed them both back into the ground is a consequence under which we all still live. Death is what we attempt most to discount, and yet all meet in time. We're guaranteed a 100% mortality rate. We're all terminal. We're all headed there. God's prophetic statements of warning are absolute and incontrovertible whether we acknowledge Him during our life span or not.

If God had stopped speaking right then in the garden, we would've been left in abject spiritual hopelessness. We could BELIEVE all we wanted, but it wouldn't get us anywhere. We might be like Mark Rothko, facing the inevitable, attempting to numb the pain. Though the biblical record remains for the investigating, was Rothko unaware of God's voice and God's heart for a safe way through?

So that we might gain better understanding, let's look further at what God has said about what is yet to come.

The Warnings Awaken the Promises

The very next prophetic statement that God makes comes in the following chapter of Genesis, embedded in His words to Adam and Eve after they ate the forbidden fruit. Certain hints of hope exist in God's next prophecy but they're far-horizon words.

First understand that the deceiver, who teased Eve to take and eat, didn't tell her that this knowledge she would gain from the stolen fruit would be to know good without being able to fully attain it and to know evil without having any power of victory over it.[72] The deceiver penetrated her mind with a challenge over what God had already said, offering no valid promise in his alternative. God's words were the only thing reliable in that tragedy.

God's warnings are consequential watchwords; they're cliff warnings on our trail map, set to help us make it through. We disregard His warnings at great peril.

Eve took the bait. She ignored the cliff warnings. She decided to counter God's warning with her own idea. She made a consequential decision. She decided which authority she was going to trust, and she had that choice.

But God enters the mess soon after this when He comes searching for Adam and Eve. Then follows a dialogue of questions and consequences in the narrative. God doesn't first ask, "What have you done?" though He rightly could have. Rather He asks, *"Where are you?"*[73]

Ponder the mercy in such a selected question: God took more interest in their separation from Him (*where*), than in their failure (*what* they had done). When He asked this of them, they were given the opportunity and the dignity to reflect, to consider and answer in time. God's question revealed His heart toward them even though what they'd done was grave.

The formatting of the Hebrew text changes at this point, starting in chapter 3 verse 14.[74] God, being the good teacher, the communicative parent, reaches for an aesthetic device: He chooses *verse*, an oracle or a poetic form of speaking that heightens what He wants them to grasp. It's like the paper loops I made for my kids; it's a way to show the drama in a way that may catch the heart toward understanding. Verse is indicated in the original language; this creative change of communicative style continues through the next six verses.

And this segment, from the mouth of God, reveals how the immediate and the long-range future will unfold. In this section we discover a hidden promise, and that promise is the second kind of prophetic statement: an unconditional guarantee in future tense.

God speaks of a *He* who will come. God announces this directly to the serpent who tempted and deceived Eve and says:

I will put enmity
Between you (serpent) and the woman,
And between your seed and her seed:
He shall bruise you on the head,
And you shall bruise him on the heel.[75]

God gives no indication, not even a hint of time, as to when this *He* will appear, but first there will be enmity, struggle, and hostility between seed of the serpent and seed of the woman. There's a lot of mystery here, because little else is explained.

But let's consider what's clear in this bad news/good news oracle. The bad news is the reality of enmity that's now part of our condition. But this *He*, some personified victor over the serpent, will come from the woman.[76]

So to summarize and to simplify, taking God's first and second prophecies, we have encapsulated all of biblical prophecy in these two declarations:

1. "You will surely die."
2. But "He" is coming.[77]

Many words add insight in the later prophetic record about this coming *He*, but you can take the above summary as solid introduction to the whole prophetic story.

We Have a Trail Map

The Bible is an incredible document. It spans 1500 years of history in its writing and involved the pens and the personalities of at least 40 different writers who spoke forth into at least as many as ten very different cultures.

Many skeptics like to debate the record in the Bible. They argue that accuracy can't be presumed through dictation taken by nomads or translations made by zealots. But if God wants to talk, can't He do that? Can't He draw a straight line using any crooked stick?

And if He does communicate His plan, are we listening?

The facts are written. The unfolding story about what's to come is so consistent and so specific that, if honestly examined, it strikes awe. A good portion of the prophetic words have already been fulfilled, some in stunning exactitude. Using the trail map analogy, we are still trekking along; we are somewhere in time continuing on this journey. But the journey will end; the trail map speaks of this. And the words about what is to come in the journey of history will be as accurately fulfilled as the trail points predicted earlier that we have already passed.[78]

No mortal could have compiled or foreseen with such precision throughout the progression of time what we have in the prophetic record. The words we see in the Bible about what is yet to come are hard to imagine, but they can be trusted. So we consult the trail map when we are not sure. God's words, recorded by the prophets, birth hope.

The Trail Map Unfolds

As prophecy moves through the Bible it starts gradually and then it builds. It is like the unfolding of a large map we can barely hold. Through the writings of many different recorders, most of whom never knew each other, we hear the same themes from different time periods, articulated with growing intensity and detail. The biblical prophecies collected in the Old and New Testaments were spoken and then recorded in the past. We ponder their meaning and authenticity in our present. Each prophet whose record we find in the biblical collection spoke into his present while at the same time speaking about what is to come in the future—sometimes centuries in advance of the actual events.

Therefore prophecy must be studied as something unfolding in history; it has to be examined closely and carefully. The words God gave the prophets are far-reaching and reliable, but sometimes complex. You have an amazing trail map. If you don't unfold it to know where you are and where you are going, you will only be wandering. God gives words and we can count on them, but to count on them means we have to exercise something called reliant trust, or faith—faith in the words and faith in the character of the One who spoke those words. It takes humility to do this. It's simple, but it's not easy.

Our Difficulties Reveal Our Trust

What Abraham and then all those following God did in their individual choices to trust God's words is the reverse of what Eve first chose to do at the tree. Remember, it all went wrong in the garden when Eve stood there discounting what God had said and disregarding the declarations He had made.

True biblical vision always contains statements of promise; fragments of hope. The prophets in the Bible received startling visions, but as we've already seen in the story of Noah, even in the harshest of predictions God always speaks words of rescue for those seeking Him.

And God's gift of sustaining hope is usually hard-won: we have to do the humble part of trusting that He means what He's said. God's promises must be taken for what they are: a gift to be opened and walked out. Active trust is the way through to the other side of trauma with God. Taking what He offers as true is the grace given for making it through.

We've Seen This Grace Before

To use a metaphor, living faith is going through the doorway to the ark that Noah built. Grace was the fact that such a doorway was even given. Hope is the rest found on the other side of that doorway. Going through that door, trusting that what God said was true may have felt very awkward to Noah, but the rescue God provided saved his life.

When Noah heard the prophetic warnings, built the boat, gathered the animals, and then walked through the door, he was living by faith, because so far it hadn't rained a drop. Every man and woman of real faith experiences similar tests in differing circumstances.

Real faith directly contrasts to our own way of independently operating. Faith directed at God and what He has said is the auto-save from our own crash-and-burn. The opposite of real faith isn't atheism or apathy—it's plain old "I'll do it my way" thinking.

Remember, prideful independence and faith are polar opposites according to God's view of things. God actually said this to one prophet who was struggling with what God was (and was not) doing. God's reply in the dialogue with that man made the contrast clear: "Behold, as for the proud one, His soul is not right within him; but the righteous will live by his faith."[79] God was rebuking the prophet, gently, and the prophet recorded that too.

Difficult circumstances swirling around can do good damage to our pride. In that sense, circumstances can even be a gift in disguise because they can force us to look beyond our own resources. Think of Eve. Think of Moses.

We have to face our circumstances honestly. When we admit we need to talk to God, to wait for His answer, especially when we don't like what we've already heard in His words, we're in the arena of true faith.[80]

That particular arena, by the way, doesn't usually feel all that "spiritual." Sometimes it's a lonely place to be, but that kind of trusting, even meager, is alive. And that kind of trust is in God, not in faith. It trusts the reliable One behind His words.

God gave Moses a test for identifying a true prophet: everything he says must come true.[81] Habakkuk, a very minor prophet in the record, sits in Jerusalem describing a coming horde with precision. He describes obediently what he is horrified to hear, and what his own pride shouts against.

History proved Habakkuk's dire prediction from God of the incredible destruction of

Jerusalem by the Babylonians some 20 years later.[82] God had said that the vision would not fail. And it didn't fail, down to every specific woe described in advance by God to this troubled mouthpiece of a prophet.[83]

The third and final chapter of Habakkuk's tear-stained journal is a statement of trust and prayer and further vision. Habakkuk first acknowledges what he hears from God as one does when receiving important instruction: "Copy that."

But he doesn't say it like a pilot in brisk military cadence; he admits his reception of the news but adds soberly, *and I fear.* He's quiet, he's saddened, and he makes a plea again because he's trusting again: "O LORD, revive Thy work in the midst of the years, In the midst of the years make it known; in wrath remember mercy."[84]

Habakkuk realizes that he can't do anything to stop what God told him is coming. But he also realizes, because of his faith, that One exists to whom he can appeal with a specific request for mercy. Habakkuk's fear hungers now for grace, and he asks directly for it. This is a man who knows he can ask.

Habakkuk's cry of trust is rewarded with more vision. God gives him a further view of a coming victory yet to be seen in human history. Here's where the hope part comes for Habakkuk and for everyone else who reads and relies on what this minor prophet learned from God.

Habakkuk records with specific detail what will happen when God Himself comes to fight the final battle, when *He* will finally "strike the head of the house of the evil, to lay him open from thigh to neck."[85] This is the longer view, that farthest horizon first hinted at back in Genesis 3:15 with the coming victorious "seed of the woman."

"He," this very seed, is coming!

Habakkuk is given an incredible peek into the unfolding drama of God's redemptive plan and he ends his reception of the vision with an emotional response:

> I heard and my inward parts trembled,
> At the sound my lips quivered.
> Decay enters my bones,
> And in my place I tremble,
> Because I must wait quietly for the day of distress,
> For the people to arise who will invade us.[86]

He shifts back, with these words, from the long-range vision he's just received to the more immediate trauma he's to warn of. It's as if he's saying "ok. The final end is going to be good, but very soon this plane's going down." There's no question that Habakkuk is accepting God's hard words as truth because he's looking around, assessing how he should live amidst these harsh realities. The immediate destruction that followed validated Habakkuk's vision. The later words will come just as surely.

Without God's Words We Have Nothing

Mark Rothko, who also knew despair, apparently did not know such access to the living Word-giver. Rothko saw an end but had nothing more than his own seer-like vision. He knew no way through it.

In contrast, Habakkuk's last journal entry is a determination of faith and hope. Though "the dark will swallow the red" in coming years for Habakkuk and his people, we have the record of how he lived out his trust in what will come beyond the destruction.

Habakkuk saw the far horizon with God. He believed the vision and, more importantly, still believes in the holy character of the One speaking. He ends his journal with a song, a response to the call of God.

> Though the fig tree should not blossom,
> And there be no fruit on the vines,
> Though the yield of the olive should fail,
> And the fields produce no food,
> Though the flock should be cut off from
> the fold,
> And there be no cattle in the stalls,
> Yet I will exult in the LORD,

I will exult in the God of my salvation,
The Lord God is my strength,
And He has made my feet like hinds feet,
And makes me walk on my high places.[87]

I put these words to melody so I could memorize them, walk them out, and own them in my heart even as everything else around me is growing dimmer. God's words and Habakkuk's response continually inform my own angst over things I don't like, things I can't change. God knows about these things, and I talk to Him about them, gaining real comfort. Like Habakkuk, I take courage in what God said in the midst of hard things. His words inform me, model for me how again to settle with God by looking to the future He has detailed. I pivot inside my soul.

The words layered in Scripture have stood the tests of every time. They've ignited my own life from self-absorption to a confidence I could not manufacture. Counting as true what God said builds hope in me that can't be replicated by anything the world has to offer. *He* is coming and *He* gets the last word on everything.

Warnings then Promises

God's warnings, that first kind of prophetic statement, land in time; they happen in our history. We all live through the consequences of God's warnings whether we pay attention to them or not. God's promises, on the other hand, are fertile seeds. They can fall on hard soil and bring nothing forth. But when the seed of God's promise meets a heart that receives it with trust, life blossoms forth in that soul.

Echoes of this MARKER: Prophecy

1. What's your own candid reaction to the idea of prophecy?

2. Read through a biblical prophecy below. List what is clear and anticipated after the time of this writing, then consider whether this has been fulfilled to date:

   - As Israelites entered the land: Numbers 24:1-19

   - Near the end of Moses' life: Deuteronomy 18:14-22

   - Some of what Isaiah saw in late 7th c. BC: Isaiah 53

   - What Jeremiah saw before the Babylonian invasion, 586 BC: Jeremiah 8:1-15

   - What Ezekiel also saw in the late 6th c. BC: Ezekiel 37:1-14

   - What Zechariah saw in the 5th c. BC: Zechariah chapters 12-13

   - What Simeon saw with baby Jesus: New Testament, Luke 2:21-35

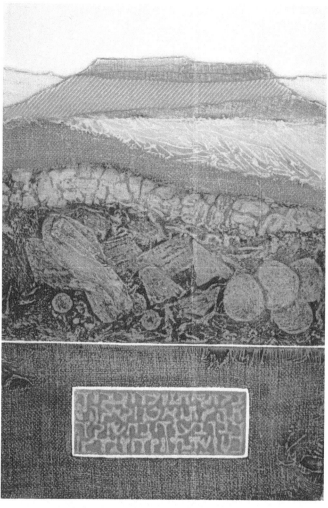

Fortress Finds by Sandra Bowden

The time was to come, when that wine too
would be spilled on the street-stones,
and when the stain of it would be red
upon many there.
Charles Dickens[88]

MARKER 5

The Promised One—Unrecognized

Where to look for this Marker: John 1:29-34;
Matthew 11:2-6 and Luke 4:16-30

One dark episode from an old science
fiction series called *The Twilight Zone* really
haunted me as a kid. The idea still does
haunt. Here's the tale: some weird-looking
aliens descended into an ordinary town. They
exited their very modern-looking spaceship
ominously and then began looking around.

The townspeople couldn't avoid the
intrusion. Everyone saw it. But they also hid
themselves in skepticism as the aliens soon
entreated anyone who would listen to enter
the spaceship. This was obviously crazy.

Time went by as some debated. The aliens
seemed gentle and had delivered a warning,
followed by a guarantee of some kind of safety.

Most of the show focused on the tension between cloistered groups of townsfolk as they argued over the aliens' intentions.

Who would be so foolish as to trust the words of weirdos and walk into that spaceship? Who had reason to fear anything until the aliens showed up? Though the creatures' offer for safety grew more and more urgent with each passing day, not one earthling ventured aboard the strange ship.

Their invitation to the crowds soon expired—time was up. No one but the aliens reentered the glistening disk. They moped slowly back inside, closed their spaceship door, and disappeared.

"Finally, they're out of here!" The townsfolk cheered relief. They congratulated themselves for their resilience.

But the story twisted with the realization, soon quite apparent, that the aliens actually had come as rescuers from an imminent danger, one that they alone understood but that the townsfolk couldn't imagine. The opportunity to be saved had come and gone. Terrible danger loomed as the story concluded, but now there was no way out.

More Fearful than an Old Story

I remember that whole episode vividly. The show is dated, but the troubling idea is not: this sense that common folk have blind spots and prejudices that can prevent them from seeing urgently what's in their own best interest.

That was just a tale. But here's something even scarier: what if the "He" God spoke of first in Genesis 3,[89] the "He" echoed by the Hebrew prophets, the "He" who would be their long-awaited rescuer, had already come? What if "He" had been predominantly dismissed and rejected? What if his blood had been spilled on the streets?

John the Baptizer actively anticipated the coming of this promised He. John, an urgent and mysterious guy, behaved like the Hebrew prophets of older times. The opening of the New Testament introduces us to his uniqueness.

John wasn't a typical Jewish townsman. He lived in the desert, wore strange clothes, and ate weird food. But his words caught people's attention. His message appealed at first, and many curious walked out of their towns to hear what John had to say. "Maybe John is a prophet speaking for God?" they wondered.

One day, near the Jordan River, John received an even greater vision. He'd already "seen" and had warned that the Kingdom was "at hand"[90] and that people needed to get ready for it by being baptized (cleansed ritually in the river's water). Then Jesus approached, also to be baptized.

John blurted a prophetic statement as he saw the approaching Jesus: "Behold the Lamb of God who takes away the sin of the world!"[91] John then exclaimed his own astonishment: "And I did not recognize Him." Later he repeats this: "And I did not recognize Him"[92] That's the way Jesus entered—he astonished even those who were expecting him.

Not long after this, King Herod threw John the Baptizer into prison. John had said things that rubbed power players the wrong way, and in the end he paid the ultimate price for his politically-incorrect boldness.

But before his head got sliced off, in prison John brooded with questions. Things weren't going as he'd expected. He'd heard about things Jesus was doing, but Jesus wasn't fulfilling everything that the Hebrew prophets had said the coming "He" would do.

Rechecking the Authority

By questioning, John did what any follower of God must do: check out the facts. John humbled himself and went to the source. He boldly pursued the truth, but he admitted also that he needed help.

So John sent a messenger directly to Jesus and asked: "Are you the Expected One, or shall we look for someone else?"[93]

John had already stated that Jesus had surprised him. We don't know what John had in mind while he actively prepared the way for the coming Messiah, but he at least admitted that Jesus didn't fit his expectations. Later, with the narrative crashing down around John, he had great reason to doubt, but he took that doubt and directed it right at Jesus.

Jesus got the message and answered immediately. He opened the trail map and quoted several prophetic promises from the biblical record. "Go and report to John what you hear and see: the blind receive sight[94] and the lame walk, the lepers are cleansed and the deaf hear, and the dead are raised up, and the poor have the gospel preached to them.[95] And blessed is he who keeps from stumbling over me."[96]

Jesus Answers the Challenge

John would've understood the significance of Jesus' reply because Jesus quoted directly from Isaiah's visions about the coming Messiah. John rightly exercises his responsibility to check Jesus out because, if for even the slightest reason Jesus wasn't that coming final Prophet, then John needed to know.

But like all the preceding prophets, John wrestled with things that remained unclear and confounding. Others looked at Jesus and wondered, "Is not this the carpenter's son?"[97] Isn't he that ordinary guy we're so familiar with?

One day Jesus visited his hometown. As was his custom, he entered the synagogue on the Sabbath and stood up to read. Jesus opened the scroll of Isaiah the prophet, turned to a certain portion, and read aloud:

> The Spirit of the Lord God is upon me,
> Because The Lord has anointed me to bring good news to the afflicted;
> He has sent me to bind up the broken hearted,
> To proclaim liberty to captives,
> And freedom to prisoners;
> To proclaim the favorable year of the Lord...[98]

And then, mid-sentence, Jesus closed the scroll and sat down. All eyes in the place fixed on him. Jesus had recited this well-known portion predicting the coming days of the Anointed One, the Messiah. But he stopped abruptly in the middle of the second verse, leaving them all waiting.

What he left out was important, but what he said next proved even more significant. He then announced to them, "Today this Scripture has been fulfilled in your hearing."[99]

This shocked his audience, and Jesus intended it to. He didn't just read Isaiah's words in the abstract as an intellectual exercise. Rather, he made a claim that what Isaiah had seen some 700 years earlier was now coming true, that very day, in their midst.

Jesus announced that these prophetic words were literally about *him*.

Rage filled those who heard him say this.[100] Imagine yourself in their sandals. ("Is this not Joseph's son?")[101] They comprehended his meaning but reacted with offense at the audacity of his claim. They should've checked him out further, as John the Baptist did in the midst of his own confusion.

Instead, the synagogue officials in Nazareth quickly drove Jesus out of town before they could experience any signs of his authentication.

John's questions moved me when I first encountered them. They rang true. John became a real personality to me; someone who aimed to follow God but found the way wasn't easy. As a God-follower myself, I'm grateful Scripture lets us in on his inner tension.

What John did with his bewilderment is significant, and it's an important takeaway from these two scenarios: take your question right to Jesus. John did, and he got his answer directly.

The Prophet Isaiah Laid the Groundwork

Both Jesus and John understood why Isaiah mattered so much to the Messiah narrative. Isaiah lived and served as a spiritual champion in Jerusalem centuries before the time of Jesus and was highly regarded for his singular moral voice during the long reigns of several Judean kings.

Isaiah's writings are the first in the Old Testament grouping of prophetic books. His writing is complex, a masterwork with rich vocabulary and imagery. The name Isaiah means "The salvation of the Lord," or "The Lord is salvation."[102] [103]

The prophetic portions woven throughout are far-reaching and though written directly to the nation of Judah, Isaiah sees broadly and covers events ahead of his time that extend worldwide in scope. Some of his predictions such as the names of future leaders and their decrees or judgments are so precise that some skeptics have concluded that someone must have edited those facts in later, long after Isaiah's death.

This assumption retreats to human prejudice and forgets or denies that God can speak through men in any time; that God knows the future. God did speak through Isaiah. Both Jesus and John respected his words, and some of Isaiah's predictions still remain to be seen in history.

The most difficult part in understanding Isaiah is locating the time-frame for the fulfillment of his prophecies, because in some sections Isaiah moves quickly from near to far vistas as if skimming over mountaintops in a fast-moving glider. Without much information as to the length of years between the events he describes, we get a big picture view from this visionary.

It must have been a wild ride for him.

In the 700 years after Isaiah recorded his visions, the Jewish nation suffered two devastating conquests, both predicted. The Jews, by the time of John the Baptizer in the first century AD, lived under the captivity of the Romans. Their longing for the foretold Hebrew deliverer remained ripe and unfulfilled.

Jesus Offers Isaiah's Promise

The portion that Jesus reads in his hometown synagogue is one of Isaiah's later chapters, a section emphasizing God's coming salvation. By his selection and the way Jesus reads the passage, he's announcing that now, in Jesus' time here on earth, God's salvation is imminent, "at hand",[104] and that the broader unfulfilled final judgments would come later.

Jesus' claims of being the fulfillment—"Do not think that I came to abolish the Law or the Prophets; I did not come to abolish but to fulfill..."[105]—were bold and repeatedly unequivocal. If Jesus had spoken presumptuously, if he'd claimed something that wasn't true, his earnest listeners had the responsibility to soundly reject him.

But if what he said *was* true, then they'd have to grapple with the heavy weight of wonder right in front of them.

And Jesus Leaves Us Waiting on the Judgment

And here's the kicker: the part that Jesus left out that day in his hometown synagogue, the part of Isaiah's prophecy he did *not* recite, was a proclamation of "the Day of Vengeance."[106] Isaiah had clearly seen that the Messiah would do the things Jesus was doing, but Isaiah also saw that the Messiah would initiate a day of terrible and final reckoning.

When Jesus makes his announcement quoting Isaiah and then hangs back mid-sentence from the judgment part of the job description, he's giving them time. He purposely stops right before the clean-up part of Isaiah's prediction.

Jesus, then, was either a false prophet by claiming Isaiah's predictions for himself and not fulfilling it all (as John had been wondering), or Jesus was offering something else. They didn't give his presentation the time it deserved for careful consideration.

There are only two options here. Jesus either was fulfillment that day of what Isaiah predicted, or he wasn't. A true prophet is not half a prophet. God gave us this measure in Deuteronomy: a prophet's words must all come true or they're all presumptuous.[107]

Jesus did everything he claimed to be doing.[108]

In the area around Galilee and Judea, many witnessed the works Jesus did that authenticated Isaiah's predictions. But it's notable that Jesus didn't recite Isaiah's words of judgment in the synagogue, and in omitting those words he remained consistent with other statements he'd made that he did not come (then) to judge.[109] He stated his mission this way: "For the Son of Man has come to seek and to save that which is lost."[110]

He intentionally did *not* say what he wouldn't then do. It seems, according to the way Jesus cites Isaiah's predictions, that there's a time lag between the first and the second parts of the sentence he reads from Isaiah 61. There's mercy space between the coming of miracles through the Messiah and a later realization of the Messiah's Day of Judgment.[111]

Isaiah's glider view merged this sentence into one event. Isaiah would've been just as surprised at Jesus as John was.

Already Seen, But Not All Accomplished

Theologians who carefully study prophetic writings have noticed a pattern in fulfillments. Oftentimes, as we saw in Genesis 3, Scripture gives little information about large gaps of time, even while waves of authenticating fulfillments keep the expectancy of final resolution alive. This pattern has been dubbed "already/not-yet," and it occurs in abundance in the particulars of the mysterious prophetic statements throughout the Bible.[112]

Remember how in Genesis 3 God promised a coming victor over the serpent, and that this victor would come from the woman's seed? Eve, likely holding to this promise, described her third son a "seed" and names him "substitute." Seth is a partial fulfillment, but more than that: Seth is actually a foreshadowing of what would fully come much later.

Seth never accomplished what God promised the final substitute would do. And even with Jesus, the full finishing of Satan is yet to come. *Already/not yet.* It seems that God, the author of the promises and the author of history, takes particular interest in revealing patterns slowly and in giving us hints of real hope all along the way.[113]

The time delay is part of the fertile ground for receiving the seed of these incredible promises. We receive what we need to know, and then we receive the opportunity to trust the One who exists beyond and above time.

The "not yet" part is where we wrestle, however. It's where we live in the tension of waiting. And it's in time yet coming where all the promises will be consummated. This is the ground for the testing of our faith. Eve, Abraham, Moses and all the others who sought God had to trust by faith that what He said was true and still coming, and so do we.

Time Gaps are Opportunity for Grace

By the time Jesus finished his first coming, he accomplished close to 50% of all the Messianic promises as "already." Jesus became the fullest answer to what Eve had foreseen in hope.

He was the complete "substitute," born of the woman. He's the final covering for sin, his own body split open to clothe our shame, as typified first in Genesis 3. There, in the Garden, God slew animals to provide covering and protection over the sin committed by Adam and Eve.

The fig leaves, the rigging of their own salvation didn't cut it. What God did, making garments for them in Eden, came at the cost of blood. Substitutes were slain. And those animal-skin cloaks foreshadowed a greater covering yet to come.[114]

Jesus accomplished the fullest act of covering. That's exactly what he came to do by his death and then his resurrection. He provided the way to God. He became the judicial sacrifice, the final lamb sacrifice as satisfaction before God for our guilt. This is the fearsome provision from which all grace is sourced, past, present, and future. It's the incredibly good news—the Gospel.

The Rest of Isaiah's Prediction is Coming

But Jesus did *not* accomplish all that the prophets promised concerning the final destruction and elimination of the serpent. The prophetic writings hinted[115] that there would be two visits by the Messiah, that he would be rejected, that this would actually be his redemptive plan, and that there would be another long time gap.

So when Jesus hangs back from announcing the Day of Vengeance in the synagogue and sits down waiting for their response, it's another signal of the grace of time given. They had opportunity to realize who it was they had right in front of them.

Consider Jesus' answer to a religious leader who, also like John the Baptist, had the courage to question him for more:

> For God did not send the Son into the world to judge the world, but that the world should be saved through Him. He who believes in Him is not judged; he who does not believe has been judged already, because he has not believed in the name of the only begotten Son of God. And this is the judgment, that the light is come into the world, and men loved darkness rather than light, for their deeds were evil...[116]

Salvation, then Judgment

Do you see the already/not yet pattern here? Jesus takes Isaiah's two themes, judgment and God's salvation, and he makes an appeal—one of mercy. "I'm saving now." Judgment is sure but will be dealt with later. Jesus gently led people by his words, his works, his stories, and his encounters to the most incredible of all claims: that he was not only the promised Messiah,[117] but that the Messiah was God Himself in the flesh.[118] The Jews eventually tried Jesus for blasphemy for such a claim.

By making these statements, Jesus was either a false messenger and an appealing liar of the highest order (and certainly therefore not a "great moral teacher"), or he actually was the promised victor, incognito, doing first things first. To really understand his claims is to be astounded. You have a significant Marker here but so often he is difficult to even see. He is so familiar or so infamous that we are all like John the Baptist who blurted, "I did not recognize Him!" Jesus often spoke about men in front of him as having eyes but not seeing.

If you too have been blind to the significance of Jesus, at least admit that you have a Marker in front of you that deserves investigation.

You can search all the available reliable records of leaders throughout human history who've made bold claims. You can study the announcements made by the founders of every religious system.

But nowhere will you find the radical clarity of the words that Jesus left with people as they wondered what to make of him. He predicted both his death and his victory after death in such specific terms that, after the shock of the events subsided, his coming and his dying became recognized as part of a predetermined redemption plan. What's more, Isaiah had seen hints of this centuries before.[119]

And nowhere will you find such consistent humility in the way he walked out his claims to the very end. Humility, you'll remember, is that strategic pivot each of us needs to make in the beginning to find our way to God.

Jesus was humility incarnate.

His humility was interwoven with uncompromising strength. Jesus was clearly no despot with his strength, but he didn't shy away from controversy either, and in many situations he drew it directly out. He told the truth. He said that *he* was the truth.[120] Let those words penetrate. That really got me. I've already indicated how hard I looked for truth apart from religion; but religion had never told me about this Jesus.

Jesus is the Best Marker of God

Growing up, I'd heard of gentle Jesus, but I'd never been exposed to his specific words about what he came to do.[121]

Religion crumbles under his words. Read his story and you'll see how he felt about religion. He spoke his harshest words to the self-righteous practitioners of "how-to-be-good" systems. He made singular claims that threatened every system even as he stayed under the radar in the way leaders usually grab headlines.

In his lifetime, he said hard things that left many troubled and waning from their prior pleasant regard of him. His presence left no one as he found them. Everywhere he went his life became a dividing point.

The gospel writers make it clear that he continually held back from prompting too much noise so that the controversies over his claims could really sink in.[122] He gave time so his radical words could do their work before the inevitable showdown to his predicted trial and crucifixion.

His announcement in the synagogue that day is a view into the mystery of time's opportunity. It hangs out there mid-sentence, lingering as people continue to decide how they'll make up their minds about this Jesus.

What Jesus offered, both then and now, is a time-lag of grace and mercy between his coming to save and his coming to judge. The judgment has been prophesied; it hangs in the air not yet realized. And please be sure you understand: Jesus owns the Day of Vengeance that Isaiah foresaw. It is yet to come, and Jesus said he will bring it.[123] [124]

At the end of Matthew's gospel, once the religious rulers officially rejected Jesus and time moved toward his death, he prepared his disciples for the sign of his second coming: "For then there shall be a great tribulation, such as has not occurred since the beginning of the world until now, nor ever shall."[125]

He gives them two whole chapters'-worth of preparative description of terrible days human history is yet to see.[126] If the prophecies that led to Jesus' first coming were so precisely fulfilled, we might expect that his words describing his second arrival won't be just symbolic urgency. Those days will be excruciatingly difficult, and Jesus warns specifically what to watch for and how to pray.

Until those days arrive and hell breaks loose, you have an opportunity for examination and reflection. Will you look to Jesus, into the very face of God's grace? Or will you run him out of your town?

He awaits a response from anyone investigating him just as he did that day in his synagogue. But one day in the future that second arrival that Isaiah and every other Bible prophet foresaw will come without delay.

Two-Thousand Years and We're Still Waiting?

It's natural for people to mock because the predicted end hasn't happened yet—easy to dismiss it as a fantasy of religious whackos. But Jesus didn't consider judgment a fantasy; he was extremely careful how he spoke of it.

I'm banking on Jesus' words, the good and the hard, because his life authenticated his every claim down to precise detail. He holds my future in his able hands. He bought it. People around the world have had millennia to consider him. That constitutes a long, long season of mercy.

The door to his ark remains open. Jesus is the embodiment of the prototype we saw prefigured with Noah. Jesus has God's favor, and if I'm related to him, I too am given this entrance of grace.

Jesus said he was "the door."[127] One day, that door will close.

Echoes of this MARKER: Jesus

1. Do some investigating into the New Testament record of Jesus:

   - His beginning: Matthew 1:1-23, John 1:1-18

   - His first teaching: Matthew, chapters 5-7

   - The way he worked: Mark 10:32-45, Luke 23:34

   - The way he handled conflict: Matthew 12:1-28

   - What he promised: John 3:14-18, John 5:24, Matthew 24:25-37

   - The way he died: Matthew 27:37-54

   - What he assured them of after the resurrection: Matthew 28:1-20, Luke 24:13-35

2. Near the end of his time with the disciples, Jesus prompted them to verbalize who they really understood him to be. (Matthew 16:13-20). In light of what you see above, make your own statement as to the identity of this man.

Touch Me, My Gargoyle Heart by
Grace Carol Bomer

Here lies the tremendous mystery that God
would be all-powerful but refuse to coerce.
Elisabeth Elliot[128]

Jesus himself did not try to convert the two
thieves on the cross; he waited until one of
them turned to him.
Dietrich Bonhoeffer[129]

MARKER 6

Choice—It's Yours

Where to look for this Marker: John 20:24-29,
Revelation 1:17-18

The fact that you've stayed with this book indicates the possibility that God has already whispered to your heart. God is walking where you're hiding and wooing your soul with "Where are you?"

This little book details a progression of Markers God gave us to know the way to safety. The journey to the God who made us begins with our humility and moves to prayer. Fear, inevitable on broken ground, can give way to grace because we've become aware of our need for rescue in Him.

But things often get hard as the journey progresses. Trusting what God has said, checking His trail map, and keeping faith in His character strengthens us to keep going.

Lastly, we come to Jesus. One New Testament writer called him God's last word—the summary in human form of all God wanted to say to men.[130] Jesus' disciple John called him the logos, or the first word.[131] The first word and the last word—both profound philosophical statements made by simple men whose lives Jesus revolutionized.

Jesus lived what he offered: a life of peace in the midst of great turmoil, a life of significance though he was so disregarded and mistreated, a life freely given to cover the sin of all mankind, and a life of eternal victory after death for those who would trust him.

He said he'd be the first, buying the way for many who would follow him into eternity. He said that he was the good shepherd who could guarantee that.[132] No other religious leader has bought your eternity with his own life. That's why Jesus is God's best Marker.

We're Left to Examine God's Best Marker

In the last book of the New Testament, Jesus' disciple John received a detailed vision of end times happenings in a book called "The Revelation of Jesus Christ."[133] John quotes what he heard from Jesus: "Do not be afraid: I am the first and the last, and the living one; and I was dead, and behold I am alive forevermore, and I have the keys of death and of Hades."[134]

Jesus claimed that the keys in his hands held each man's eternal destiny. He offers the greatest intervention, the greatest jailbreak possible by his own authority as "the living one."

I sense that time is getting tight toward the days of tribulation of which Jesus warned. God hasn't given me some secret vision about the timing of the future, but as an artist I feel a deep tug in my heart when I see people flitting aimlessly, when I see increasing signs, and when I see so many despairing as Mark Rothko did.

I've read the really hard words that many of the prophets and Jesus said about the last days on earth. God gave these warnings not to scare but to advise and prepare the hearers. When describing the final judgments, some of the prophets became physically sick from their encounters with the visions.[135] But even as it was when Jesus walked among men, many today remain uninterested in the mounting signs around us.

We Can Craft Our Own Idea—For a While

A friend of mine, referring to a line from a poem, once stated that the phrase "unruly man, a violent God"[136] wasn't his idea of God. I wished for a moment that I too could insist on my own idea of God. That way I could maybe be insulated from pain.

But I can't. Pain encircles me, resides within me, and so it is for my friend.

To craft an idea of God that doesn't address the problem of our pain is no god at all. God has entered into pain, felt pain deeply, and He has made a way *through* pain. No crafted god does that, has done that, or can do that.

What's more, the prophetic record indicates that life on earth won't end in a rosy way. Life experience already betrays such delusion. Those rocked by the tsunami in Indonesia, or the earthquake in Sichuan, or any number of other disasters have to decide where they stand with a God who is either violent or absent or...what?

Any of these options—that He's capriciously violent, that He's impotent or uncaring, or that He simply doesn't exist— may leave people feeling better in the short term, but in the long run all these postulations lack any real help for souls.

We Need Help

C.S. Lewis, when trying to illustrate to his readers who his Christ character Aslan was, said, "He is not safe...but He is good."[137] In other words, God won't perform the way you want. He'll do things you won't understand, but He's good, completely and faithfully in everything that comes down.

When trauma comes, we behave like frightened deer who don't know which way to run for safety. He's the best option. Run to Him, even though it's frightening to turn to Him, especially when you're unsure. His character is open for the examining. The writer of the vision in Revelation describes Him coming to wage the final battle, and his name is "Faithful and True."[138]

Another friend of mine said, "But Mary, I just can't believe."

Sadly, I understand that, too. Once, when faith was offered to me, I mocked it. I needed more reasons.

But as I thought about my friend's objection, I wondered, "How could I help her believe? How does anyone actually decide to believe? How did I ever believe?"

And then the words came flooding into me: "Faith comes from hearing, and from hearing by the word of Christ."[139] That means if we humble ourselves (Eve pivot) and read what Jesus said in the record, we receive content about God's best Marker—a Marker we can truly rely on.

Another friend found herself reading the words of Jesus in a hotel Bible and simply recognized "I need a friend like that." That was her beginning.

Offer your heart a chance to consider the One who still speaks. Remember Jesus when he said the words from the text and then waited in his synagogue for their response. He waited. God has spoken many times in many ways and His final word is Jesus. Faith isn't some blind leap into an imaginary land—it's a decision based on what God has said and what He did through Jesus. Understanding Him is what all the other Markers lead to. He called Himself the Shepherd. He's your soul Sherpa on Everest and beyond. Maybe you did not know you needed him, but you won't make it without him.

As It Was in the Beginning

We circle back to the Garden with this one. You stand before the tree and other influences toss multitudes of alternatives at you. Will you listen to what God said and trust that He means it?

This is the great mystery: God leaves this eternal decision up to each of us. If you look at the first two chapters of Genesis, you'll see God very active, very involved, and very verbal. The contrast is all the more confounding when, in the third chapter, Eve stands debating before the tree. God is nowhere to be seen, nor can He be heard for the first seven verses of that turning-point chapter.

When I first observed this, God's silence really bothered me. He hangs back while she decides. You can search the record for yourself. In the whole of the Bible, God offers, He speaks, He pleads through the prophets, but then sometimes He goes silent.[140] Jesus offers, he speaks, and he weeps, but nowhere does he constrain anyone. And then he too goes silent.

One day while Jesus walked from town to town, a young seeker came and asked him a key question: "What shall I do to inherit eternal life?"

They discussed what the first prophet, Moses, had already laid out. This inquirer claimed that he followed the rules "from his youth up." Jesus looked at him and "felt a love for him." Then he responded.

"One thing you lack..." Jesus seemingly had particular knowledge of this man and his circumstances. The 'rule-following' wasn't enough, and Jesus gets at the heart with his answer to the man's earnest query.[141]

The man heard Jesus' reply. "But at these words his face fell, and he went away grieved for he owned much property."

This amazed the disciples. They had already made a decision to follow, yet when they saw the mystery and difficulty of following played out in front of them they exclaim, "Who then can be saved?"

Jesus answers that question also: "With men it is impossible, but not with God; for all things are possible with God."[142]

God can do the impossible and He can do it however He wants, but He leaves the issue of trusting Him up to us. He hangs back and waits. Some choose to follow Him. Some walk away. It's been that way, as we've seen, from the very beginning.

We Have a Significant Choice

It's hard to square with the idea that one can actually engage with the God of Creation and get right in His face. But we can—through Jesus. God came in the form of this gentle rabbi to communicate with us—to share His love for us.

We can dismiss him, decide not to recognize his mercy, and walk away. He'll let us do that. He'll let us be in charge. But we at least need to understand what that choice involves.

One night in my dorm room an unusual set of events made it clear to me that Jesus was who he said he was: the radical, reckoning, reaching God of my soul. This decisive moment, frankly, wasn't fun. But it was what I'd been looking for: the truth about eternal issues.

I had this heavy sense that I could walk away, and that if I did, I'd be running from Jesus the rest of my life. That night I made my first Eve Pivot, and I began to learn to pray. Forty-seven years since that decision, I have never once regretted making it. I'm a wrestler,

I'm a big-time struggler, God knows. But my soul has found its rest in Him.

And He Will Meet Us There

Jesus' crucifixion blindsided his disciples and they all scattered. All their hopes in His Messianic claims hung and died on that cross along with him. A few days later, one of the disciples, a man named Thomas received reports from the others that Jesus was actually alive again.

Hope is irritating when you've decided something can't be true. For Thomas, this was weird and probably more than irritating. Even though Jesus told them several times that this would happen, they couldn't comprehend it. It was unbelievable. Thomas was too emotionally invested and then devastated to hope, and that's a hellish place to be.

But his story doesn't stop there. Thomas countered his friends: "Unless I see for myself the imprint of the nails in His hands, and put my own finger in the place of the nails, and put my hand into where His side was cut open, I will not believe."[143]

"I'm adamant," says Thomas, but somehow he's still hanging around eight days later, and then Jesus shows up. After greeting them all, Jesus goes directly to Thomas and says: "Reach here your finger, and see my hands; and reach here your hand, and put it into my side; and be not unbelieving but believing."[144]

Jesus leaves that believing response in our court. Think of Judas. He sat at the table too, but then he walked away. This is a fearful thing: the decision for our allowing the rescue of our eternal destiny rests in our response to Jesus.

He's a gentleman. He won't coerce you with His offer of rescue. But He is God and He can fully save you if you ask Him to. Remember, He has the keys in *His* hands.[145]

So Jesus accommodates them both. The man who walks away isn't stopped, not chased after. He has full freedom to make his own choice. And the man who needs more to believe is directly and specifically supplied.

It depends on what you want.

Oxford Scholar C.S. Lewis, who decided late in life to follow Jesus, laid out his own choice this way so that others could understand:

If you want to get warm you must stand near the fire: if you want to be wet you must get into the water. If you want joy, power, peace, eternal life, you must get close to, or even into, the thing that has them. They are not a sort of prize, which God could, if He chose, just hand out to anyone. They are a great fountain of energy and beauty spurting up at the very center of reality. If you are close to it, the spray will wet you: if you are not you will remain dry. Once a man is united to God, how could he not live forever? Once a man is separated from God, what can he do but wither and die?[146]

There's something critical about the dignity of this choice. True love gives this freedom even as it grieves when so many walk away. And please understand, this isn't just an offer from 'gentle Jesus, meek and mild.' It's an offer from God who has paid for your eternal freedom, an offer that covers you from coming judgment over the consequences of sin.

What Jesus offers and gives is always more than you understand. Remember John the Baptizer's learning curve? John had to adjust his expectations even as he had vision from God. He had to probe for more. He took his questions to Jesus.

Anglican theologian John Stott emphasizes what John saw in the desert: "Because the good news of the gospel is that God takes our sinfulness into Himself; and overcomes in His own heart what cannot be overcome in human life."[147] He takes your sin and shortcomings seriously, enough to carry them to death for you.

In the end, how you respond to Jesus is your soul's most consequential decision.

Echoes of this MARKER: Choice

1. If God exists, is all-powerful, why would human choice even matter?

2. A choice is highlighted in each of these stories. Read to identify it:

   - Joshua: Joshua 24:1-28

   - Ruth: Ruth 1:1-18

   - David: Psalm 39

   - Solomon: 2 Chronicles 1:1-13

   - Jonah: Jonah chapters 1-2 (there are several choices going on here)

   - Samaritan woman at the well: New Testament, John 4:7-30

   - Peter at Pentecost: New Testament, Acts 2:14-40

Banished by Kareem Blake

Why does death so catch us by surprise, and why love? We still and always want waking.
Annie Dillard[148]

MARKER 7

Forever—God's Promise

*Where to look for this Marker: Genesis 16:7-8
and 1 Peter 1:3-5*

The best stories keep on going. The
trouble with ours is that each of our stories
eventually ends. A New Testament verse says
that because our deaths are certain, we
operate as slaves, cowering in fear of what
could be coming and what is ending.[149]

As the rock singer and poet Jim Morrison
said, "Nobody gets out of here alive."[150] We're
captives in time. It comes for every single one
of us. The ancient warning from Genesis gets
personally consummated: "you shall surely
die."

The last Marker on our journey is a Trail's
End sign. It's where you get to stop; it's what
you've been walking toward. Some come to

this end point early, some late. But Morrison and any other wise guy, secular or religious, has little to say about what comes next after that.

Is This It?

Years ago, a high school friend called to give me news of a buddy we knew who had died in a head-on collision. My friend, who doesn't share my convictions about God's reliability, wrestled with the idea that this could be all that there is for our friend Scott, now gone.

"What does 'deceased' mean?" he asked. "How can the substance of someone's unique existence suddenly evaporate?"

There's a mournful song that encapsulates this and concludes with only the question:

Is that all there is?[151]

God's story provides a real answer. His begins in a perfect place, hand-built by Him. The heavens and all matter start functioning progressively in time. More specific detail is available in the Genesis account about His crafting of a beginning than you can find in any other sacred literature.

What anyone chooses to embrace about origin will impact how he views himself. If you yield to the possibility that a Being beyond time initiated who you are, then your identity certainly adjusts.

Wishful thinking? God's self-evaluation after creating man and woman was that His handiwork was "very good." That's *His* stated view on each new life and we unconsciously agree, in spite of any prior denials about the supernatural, when we look into the purity of a newborn's face. There's something very deep about this instinct of origin. There is something really good echoing here.

As the Genesis story progresses into particular histories, we learn of a slave woman named Hagar from Abraham's household. Abraham's wife Sarah didn't consider Hagar "good" so Sarah treated her harshly. Hagar flees into the desert where "an angel of the Lord" finds her.

Hagar has a life-changing encounter with this supernatural being who asks two questions:

"Where have you come from and where are you going?"[152]

The questions search her soul and indicate value in her personal story—that began in one place but will end in another.

Hagar decides from this encounter that God sees and that He views her intimately and knowingly.[153] This revolutionized her thinking. She is honored as the only woman in the book of Genesis who is assured, "do not fear".[154] More than that, she is honored as the only woman in all of Scripture who assigns a name to this God who sees. She, an outcast, had a significant encounter with the One who saw her.

More Than Where We Are Now

Hagar was on a journey. It felt bleak to her, to be sure, but God knew that she was going somewhere. He connected with her where she was so that she too could grasp this.

In Genesis, after the tragedy in the Garden, after God seeks out the hiding sinners, after He pronounces resulting sorrows and a future plan, He covers them.

And then God casts them "out from the garden of Eden"[155] where we all end up acting like slaves, where death stalks us, where we work hard to construct our own gardens and come short every single time.

But God's entry into every story in His book indicates that more exists. In so many ways He reveals a progressive outworking, hinting that forever is real beyond what anyone can see here and now.

In that Genesis account of our being cast outside, God gives a reason: man and woman are removed and barred from re-entry "lest he (man) stretch out his hand, and take also from the tree of life and live forever."[156]

Living forever was a possibility right from the beginning, but God kept it decisively out of our reach. Forever-life taken from that tree then would've meant our being locked in disobedience eternally. Forever marred. So God kept forever from us, and that removal was costly. Costly for us. Costly for God.

But God's story doesn't terminate. The tree of Life existed then and still exists even though we can't access it. Forever was in the plan all along, but for us it feels like only a wish.

It's like catching a glimpse of a perfectly lit world through a fissure at the bottom of a deep well, but to get there you have to die first. Many magical stories begin with such a quest, and these epics and fantasies mirror what God already set in place.

God has a forever place. He hints at it all the way through the Bible. His true desire is for us to be with Him there, but Holiness has requirements.

Glimpses of Forever in Beauty

As a young girl, I remember waiting all dressed up by a group of suitcases on a train platform. I had no idea what was coming. Suddenly a Zephyr train slid heavily in on the tracks just beyond us. Imposing. Noisy. Incredibly gleaming. My mother and siblings stood nearby, but I endured this terror alone.

I remember being riveted. I remember trying to gather what color this beast was. I knew no crayon in my box could replicate what loomed in front of me.

Time collapses for me when I think of how that felt—it was transfixing. I'm searching for words now. Why did I search then for a crayon in my child-mind? That experience was a first indicator for me of the existence of awe, and already I was considering that it might be possible to capture it.

I have since learned that artists and philosophers are still trying to articulate their experiences with beauty. Some writers explore how hints of terror often come alongside such beauty.

Beauty is elusive. It is fleeting and often subjective. When someone cries, "Oh, that's so beautiful!" they're responding with pleasure. But, if pressed, they won't be able to adequately explain why. Beauty silently ushers you to an impression, and then the knowing disappears.

I think beauty is a glimpse of forever that keeps us moving forward in time. It's a beckoning gift. Forever is eternal and for us that's abstract. We are temporal and concrete, but beauty is a sign that there is a forever place. Like a wooing melody. Like shimmering dewdrops on a pile of straw. Maybe moments of beauty are like vista points along a hike— those few places that make the whole arduous walk worth it because we get to see through to what is "out there", where it is we are really going.

Yet this beauty view is utterly un-capture-able. That's its nature. Beauty is a signifier, like a supernatural whiff of God. It is a manifestation of our inner desire and, according to what I see in Scripture, of His desire for us. But like the tree of Life, we can't own it fully here.

This unattainable aspect of beauty explains why my soul aches when I encounter it. An artist whom I admire describes it this way: " ...every time you see beauty, along with that beauty comes that sense of disappointment of life passing."[157]

Yes, something about our mortality limits our access. My soul longs for beauty, is saddened by its fleeting nature, and desires to know more. Beauty is a glimpse of forever.

Maybe this sense of forever along the way is the better Marker, not my trail's end sign. It's the beauty I will be remembering in the days after my trail's end. It's the beauty Marker that I then need to heed, for it suggests to my heart that where my feet are on this ground is not all there is.

Words of Forever in the Old Testament

We see forever's beautiful call at the beginning of God's story, we see it in the end, and we can see glimpses of it all along the way.

God called Abraham to a nomadic life and progressively gave him more and more promises about what was to come. Abraham believed God and invested his life trusting that much, much more was coming than what he had tangibly in front of him, "for he was looking for the city which has foundations, whose architect and builder is God."[158] God gave Abraham the content for such a visual dream and kept him walking toward it.

Job, a character early on in the biblical story, was greatly tested by God. At the beginning of Job's 42-chapter epic, we see the throne room of heaven where God initiates a challenge with Satan over Job's integrity.

Like a five-act play, the scenes switch back and forth from decisions in this throne room to resultant trauma on earth. God describes Job at the outset as "blameless, upright, fearing God and turning away from evil."[159] But the book is long because Job's struggle is intimately excruciating.

Job blurts and he blames with sarcasm. Job is like a dog with a bone, only the bone is God. He can't give up his exhausting struggle with God's unseen purpose, and he rails. At one point Job exclaims, "Oh that my words were written! Oh that they were inscribed in a book!" (They are—we're reading them now.) "That with an iron stylus and lead they were engraved in the rock forever!" Then Job catches his breath and looks further by faith. "And as for me, I know that my Redeemer lives, and at the last He will take His stand on the earth."[160]

We already saw this idea of the Redeemer coming "at the last" hinted in God's words of promise from the Garden. The prophets added layer upon layer of increasing revelations of what was to come, who was to come, how *he* would come, and what would be restored as a result.

The trail map is detailed as it moves through time and human history. God-followers take the direction laid down seriously. God-followers, just like Job, spend a lot of their pride, and often a lot of pain trusting that God means what He has already said. And, they keep holding in their hearts that beauty of what is yet ahead.

Moses met God at the burning bush, then led the Hebrews out of their slavery to a land God had promised them. The Exodus story is a picture in miniature of the grand narrative in the whole of the Bible: Promise, Rescue, Doubt, the Provision of God, and finally the Presence of God.

At the end of Moses' part of the journey, he ascends to a high point over the Promised Land. There God Himself points out all the Promised Land's contours. It must have been beautiful.

God then says to him, "This is the land which I swore to Abraham, Isaac and Jacob saying, 'I will give it to your descendants.' I will let you see it with your eyes, but you shall not go over there."[161]

Moses had to "wait" until after his death to experience the fullest restoration of that land. God allowed him to see it as a foretaste of so much more to come. God's promises remain even when our bodies lay in dust awaiting fullness.

We are finite, but the inventor of forever is not.

God gave King David many promises, and his trust in God produced many heartfelt songs and poems that we call Psalms. Speaking of the afflicted and those who seek God, David says, "let your heart live forever!"[162]

We all might wish that. We were made to long for that, I believe. David knew it. "The Lord sat as King at the flood: Yes the Lord sits forever."[163] David speaks of past and present, and in the next verse—future. David recognized that God exists beyond time, over time, and will move in time toward a great finish.

"And as for me, you will maintain my just cause, and you will cause me to stand in your presence forever."[164]

Like every other human, David died and was buried. Was this promise only a false hope from an ancient poet? Stay tuned. David saw it from afar. "Surely God will shatter the head of His enemies, the hairy crown of him who goes on in his guilty deeds. The Lord said 'I will bring them back from Bashan. I will bring them back from the depths of the sea...'"[165]

Fast-forward to the Old Testament prophet Malachi. He concludes the Hebrew Scriptures with words about a coming "day" which the Creator is preparing. There was a grand beginning. There will be a grand end, but we aren't there yet. The idea of this day coming is all over the prophetic literature.

God had given several other prophets a view of this.[166] Here are Malachi's words on that future:

> For behold, the day is coming, burning like a furnace; and all the arrogant and every evil doer will be chaff; and the day that is coming will set them ablaze," says the Lord of Hosts, "so that it will leave them neither root nor branch. But for you who fear My name the sun of righteousness will rise with healing in its wings; and you will go forth and skip about like calves from the stall.[167]

More is coming, and the promised son of David assures it.[168]

Words of Forever in the New Testament

Jesus also had much to say about this coming "day." He gave his followers many words so they could hang on in the meantime.

Meantime. A better word has never been invented for time because it would be for them (and for us) a very 'mean time'. After Jesus told them he was going to die, he went on:

> Let not your heart be troubled. You are trusting God, now trust in me. There are many homes up there where my Father lives, and I am going to prepare them for your coming. When everything is ready, then I will come and get you, so that you can always be with me where I am. If this weren't so, I would tell you plainly. And you know where I am going and how to get there."
> "No, we don't," [one of them countered], "We haven't any idea where you are going, so how can we know the way?" Jesus told him, "I am the Way—yes, and the Truth and the Life. No one can get to the Father except by means of me.[169]

Later, even while hanging on the cross, Jesus gave a promise to another who turned to him and simply pled as they both were dying, "Remember me." Jesus replied, "Truly I say to you, today you will be with me in Paradise."[170] To promise someone paradise while they both hung on a cross is either a great cruelty or an incredible assurance of more.

The crucifixion shattered the disciples. The resurrection literally transformed them; they were now witnesses of forever. Jesus made eternity's safe passage a possibility for all of us.

The Promise of Forever

Forever is the last Marker, not death. The Trail's End sign gives way to an unending vista. God offers the tree of life: Jesus on the cross, "that whoever believes may in Him have eternal life."[171]

The disciples and many others who followed did a 180 and invested their own lives in something beyond physical death. Peter, who three times denied Jesus in fear, turns around and encourages others:

> What a God we have! And how fortunate we are to have him, this Father of our Master Jesus! Because Jesus was raised from the dead, we've been given a brand-new life and have everything to live for, including a future in heaven—and the future starts now! God is keeping careful watch over us and the future. The Day is coming when you'll have it all—life healed and whole.[172]

The Bible's last book, Revelation, ends with Jesus describing an ominous end on earth that the world has not yet seen. But after that, we who have responded are granted access to a place of rest, a new Garden made for us where trees give healing, and tears are wiped away. "Blessed is he who reads and those who hear the words of the prophecy, and heed the things which are written in it; for the time is near."[173]

It's important to understand that forever is for everyone. Forever is ahead for those who heed and also for those who do not. God offered a rescue plan in Jesus, but He also made it clear that His offer not taken doesn't exempt one from experiencing forever. Your Forever will be as you chose it: with Him in peace, or without Him in torment. "He who rejects me, and does not receive my sayings, has one who judges him; the word that I spoke is what will judge him at the last day."[174]

The Question Remains in Time

So the questions that the angel asked Hagar are still very relevant for each one of us: where have you come from, and where are you going?

I love a simple prayer my husband found on a website recently, refreshing for its brevity: "God, I really don't know who you are, and I don't know how to find you, but if you are God and if you are there, then you know how to find me."[175]

You already heard that finding God is a possibility. After all, He came first to find Adam and Eve in the Garden. "Where are you?" And, He came for me. His mercy could be true for you, and He is still looking.[176] If you pray, He will hear and He will know it.

If you'll hold on to me for dear life, says God,

I'll get you out of any trouble.

I'll give you the best of care

if you'll only get to know and trust me.

Call me and I'll answer,

be at your side in bad times;

I'll rescue you, then throw you a party.

I'll give you a long life,

give you a long drink of salvation!

Psalm 91:14-16 MSG

Echoes of this MARKER: Forever

1. Look into any of these passages to gain understanding of the vista beyond. Do you see anything that indicates how the one given the vision had such confidence?

   - Job, 19:7-29
   - Moses, Deuteronomy 32:1-43
   - David, 2 Samuel 7:1-17
   - Isaiah, chapter 40
   - Daniel, 7:1-16
   - Ezekiel, 1:22 through to chapter 2:2
   - Malachi, chapter 3
   - Hebrews, New Testament: chapter 1
   - Peter, New Testament: 2nd Peter 3:3-18
   - Revelation, New Testament: 21:1 through to 22:16

2. According to these words:

   a. Psalm 33:13-15, Where is God and what is He doing now, present tense?

   b. John 14:1-3, Hebrews 7:24-27, Where is Jesus and what is He doing now?

3. Where are you, and what are you doing now?

Lazarus by Barbara Februar

Epilogue

My story began after death. A girl took my place and her physical life ended. That's when my real life began.

Yes, I was living before that accident. I was breathing and thinking, had come out of a certain family, with my own history and personality. But death awoke my soul. Death started me on my search for God, and soon after I found another Jewish friend who also willingly took my place. His name is Jesus.

Your story is uniquely different. I don't know what it is, but I know it's interesting. I know you too harbor questions and tensions, fears and sorrows, but in this way you're not unique. We live these unfinished things out in time, and time reveals our story, chapter by chapter. Not everything comes at once, and this is a great mercy.

God's story gets understood in our own time too, or it can. He's given us a record; we call it the Bible, which is a collection of many stories. If succinct steps make a better way for you to understand the Bible's important messages, then you may appreciate the progression of my chapters: Humility, Prayer, Fear and Grace, Hope, Truth in Jesus, Choice, and Forever.

Start into the big story yourself. Then He can speak directly and personally to you. There's life in His words. Peace.

Jesus said that man can't live by physical food alone but needs the words that come from the mouth of God for survival. (Deuteronomy 8:3, Matthew 4:4). God is a communicator and a seeker, and that's just the beginning fringe of His character. You can find this out for yourself in ways particular to you, in ways that He designed to meet your deepest needs.

Suggestions for Finding a Bible and Beginning

Here are some things that might help orient you to God's book: go to any store or site that offers Bibles.[177] Choose one, open it up and look at the language of the text. Pick any place in the book and read a couple paragraphs.

Scholars work to translate Bibles from the original languages into readable form. You'll find that older versions like the King James translation are reliable but the language is archaic. Other more modern versions like the New King James, New American Standard, or the New International Version are solid choices.

The Living Bible and The Message are great paraphrased versions, which employ a more conversational approach. Ask questions, do your own research, and find one that reads comfortably to you. Then just start in.

Don't get uptight about which version you choose. If God really is a communicator, can't

He speak through any version? He can speak through Socrates or Moby Dick if He wants to, or through a sign in an antique shop. But the words in His text are supernatural, full of meaning, and can cut right into your soul with substance.[178]

He has spoken directly to me and to millions of others through His words. Simply place yourself under Him with a heart that wants to know. Think of it as an Eve Pivot. Begin your own silent prayer, and trust that He wants you to know Him.

The Bible is divided into two major sections that Christians called the Old Testament and the New Testament. Jews use only the Old Testament, which they call the Tanakh. In this Hebrew portion you'll find three major divisions:

1. The History
2. The Writings (Psalms and poems)
3. The Prophets

The historical books start with Genesis and move through the history of ancient Israel. The flow, because it's a big story, is mostly chronological. It's full of the events of individuals and nations. There's so much of value in there, but some parts will raise questions too.

Realize that you're looking into ancient cultures. Approach the text with the same attitude of respect you'd employ as a visitor on foreign soil. Hold your judgment with some humility. If you look for the character of God through all of this, you'll find more than you can imagine.

You'll find large histories, like Exodus or the Chronicles, and smaller histories like the love story of Ruth or the story of Esther in Persia.

Five books, more poetic and emotional in style follow the histories. I like to think of these as the "heart" of the book. In fact, if you take a Bible that has both the Old and New Testament in it and open it to the center, you'll be in this section. These five "heart books" dive directly into the inner life of several God followers. Job's epic tale of suffering is in this section. The Psalms share songs written through every imaginable struggle. The Proverbs detail sayings of timeless wisdom for relationships. Ecclesiastes contains philosophical musings, and the Song of Solomon is about romantic love and so much more.

These five books occur chronologically and are the outcome of the unique wrestlings of the writers themselves. They speak widely to everyman. Here's an example. Using Psalm 131 as a template, I recorded my own thoughts in my journal with these words:

Oh, living God. Oh, Master of me,
When I look to you again,
That very moment you cancel the independence of
my stubborn self-will;
My eyes fill with your light, my distress melts.

I am quieted, realizing that I need not,
I cannot
Take the lead in these things
that are too much for me.
These things are great matters
that I ponder...

But You; You tell me that you
hold all things together.
And you hold me!
Truly. Truly, by turning to you again,
You compose my soul.
I am like a weaned child,
still loved but still longing.
You are like a caring Mother
who recognizes my deepest need
And simply picks me up to shelter me close.
My soul is like this within me.
You are like her all around me.

Oh, God-seekers!
Take your true hope in such a God!
May today, this very time that you have,
be this for you too.
All the way to eternity. (Psalm 131, in my own words)

After the heart books comes the last
section of the Old Testament: books written by
the prophets concerning the things to come.

They number 17 in total. Some are huge works (Major Prophets), and some are tiny (Minor Prophets). Many of these give historical data and record personal struggles, but God gave these writings through the context and style of each prophet to warn and prepare the hearers for that which had not yet occurred in their history.

THE BIBLE					
Old Testament			New Testament		
History	Heart	Prophecy	History	Practical	Prophecy
17 Books	5 Books	17 Books	5 Books	21 Books	1 Book

The New Testament can be subdivided into three basic sections as well: History, Practical Instruction, and Prophecy. Its authors completed the entire New Testament by the end of the first century, and it was written in Greek, the main language of that time.

The four gospels that open the New Testament, as well as the book of Acts, document the history of Jesus' life and the early life of newborn Christianity right after Jesus left earth. In the middle section, the Practical Instruction, we find the letters of

Paul and others. The very last book is Prophecy, the Revelation written by John, the last living disciple of Jesus.

My own quest began with the possibility that one man I'd heard of, Abraham, loved God. I'm on my own walk now, learning to love God myself. This is an astounding adventure—much more satisfying and much more difficult than anything I could have traded for.

It's a lifelong journey and in the process I've stopped to really take in how much He loves me... and how much He loves you. If you get nothing else from my little book, please begin to consider the possibility of this.

He is faithful and true.

APPENDIX: Jesus and Prophecy; what has been fulfilled, what is yet to come

ALREADY: what has been fulfilled
Scholars have added up the Old Testament references that have been fulfilled by Jesus' first coming: there are over 350 of them. This chart highlights some key ones. The mathematical probability that any man could fulfill, let alone even arrange these markers is beyond possible.

	FORSEEN	*ACCOMPLISHED*
WHO: His lineage: Victor from the tribe of Judah, "Shiloh"= one sent	Genesis 49:8-12	Matthew 1:1-16; Luke 3:23-38; John 1:41, 45, 6:29, 8:42; 1 Corinthians 15:56-57
Messiah will be a Savior who is both God and Man	Jeremiah 23:5-6; Isaiah 7:14, 9:6, 43:11-13, 45:21-22, 59:16, 63:5; Zechariah 12:10	John 1:1, 8:58, 10:28-30, 13:13, 20:28

	FORSEEN	*ACCOMPLISHED*
WHAT: Seed of Abraham who blesses the nations	Genesis 12:3; Isaiah 60:1-3	Matthew 1:1; Luke 2:29-32; John 10:16 12:20-24; Galatians 3:8,16
Mysterious perpetual Priest of Peace, who offers bread and wine	Genesis 14:17-20; Psalm 110:4	Matthew 26:26-29; John 14:19,27; Hebrews 5:9,10
Provision for the Sacrifice: Lamb of God, who covers sin	Genesis 22:8, Leviticus 17:11	John 1:29, John 19:30; Matthew 1:21; Hebrews 9:22-24; Revelation 5:2-10
The ladder to heaven	Genesis 28:12	John 1:51, 14:6
Final Prophet after Moses from the Jews, who will have God's words in his mouth	Deuteronomy 18:18-19	John 1:45, 6:14, 8:28,29; Revelation 1:17-18; 22:18
King: descendant through David's line who will reign forever	2 Samuel 7:12-17; Psalm 2:6-7; Jeremiah 23:5; Micah 5:2	Matthew 1:1, 6, 2:6, 12:23, 21:9, 27:37, 28:18-20; John 18:37; Luke 1:32,33

	FORSEEN	*ACCOMPLISHED*
WHEN: timing of His arrival	Daniel 9:24-26	Galatians 4:4-5 (extra-Biblical calendar work using Daniel's markers ties precisely to the pre-Passover entry of Jesus to Jerusalem in 33AD)[179]
WHERE: Born in Bethlehem	Micah 5:2	Matthew 2:1-6
Executed, "cut off" in Jerusalem	Daniel 9:25-26; Zechariah 9:9-10	Matthew 21:1-5; John 12:10-16
WHY: God's pre-determined plan: to save	Psalm 118:22-25; Proverbs 8:22-36	Luke 19:10; Matthew 20:28; John 3:16, 10:10, 12:46,18:37; 1 Peter 1:20
HOW: Forsaken, not believed, mocked, pierced, crucified, went willingly	Psalm 22; Isaiah 53:8-11; Matthew 26:2; Mark 14:27	Matthew 26:20-27:54; Mark 14:32-15:39; Luke 22:1-23:48; John 18:1-19:35

	FORSEEN	ACCOMPLISHED
His Resurrection	Psalm 118:16-18; Isaiah 53:8-11; Matthew 20:17-19; Mark 10:32-34; Luke 18:31-34	Matthew 28:1-20; Mark 16:1-20; Luke 24:1-53; John 20:1-31
Sends forth indwelling Spirit	Proverbs 1:23; Isaiah 44:3; Jeremiah 31:31-33; Joel 2:28-29; John 14:16-17, 16:7-13; Acts 1:8	Acts 2:1-18; 1 Corinthians 2:12, 3:16; Romans 8:15-16

ALREADY/NOT YET: what lingers partly fulfilled

This is a sampling, amongst many, of predictions that have begun with ongoing fulfillments, some are one-time events that have happened as a forerunner signaling a much greater event still to come according to the full vision given.

	FORSEEN	NOW REALITY/ BUT YET TO BE FULLY REALIZED
"I see Him, but not now, I behold Him but not near…"	Numbers 24:17-19	He exists, is seen millennia before His coming: there are hints here to His first advent; also words of His final victory
"And I will put enmity between you and the woman, between your seed and her seed; He shall bruise you on the head and you shall bruise him on the heel."	Genesis 3:15	Gen.3:15; Habakkuk 3:13a is accomplished: Hebrews 2:14; However, Habakkuk 3:11,12,13b and 14 are yet to come: Revelation 19:11-21

	FORSEEN	*NOW REALITY/ BUT YET TO BE FULLY REALIZED*
"You meant evil against me, but God meant it for good in order to bring about this present result, to preserve many people alive"	Genesis 50:20, full story starting in chapter 37	The story of Joseph rejected and left for dead by his brothers typifies God's intervention at that time; it also foreshadowed Christ's rejection by His countrymen; and also looks to the future's restoration: Zechariah 12:10; Revelation 1:7
No end to the increase of His government	Isaiah 9:7a; Numbers 24:19a; Zechariah 9:9-10; Matthew 28:18; John 17:2,24-26	His dominion has begun in some hearts; His Kingdom is "at hand;" yet a full Kingdom is yet to be realized on earth. Amos 9:11-15; Zechariah 9:14-17

	FORSEEN	NOW REALITY/ BUT YET TO BE FULLY REALIZED
Darkness signs in sky before the terrible day of the Lord	Joel 2:30-31	Peter, quoting Joel in Acts 2:19-20 is referring to the darkness that happened mid-day during the crucifixion: Matthew 27:45; but the last days predictions anticipate a much more cataclysmic darkness coming: Matthew 24:29, Joel 2:30-31, 3:9-17; Revelation 16:10
Jewish Temple destroyed by "people of the prince who is to come"	Daniel 9:26-27; Matthew 24:1-2, and 15; Mark 13:2; Luke 19:43,44; 2 Thessalonians 2:3-4	The Roman General Titus destroyed Herod's temple in 70AD, foreshadowing another expected temple destruction: Revelation 11:1-7; Isaiah 66:1-6

	FORSEEN	NOW REALITY/ BUT YET TO BE FULLY REALIZED
All the nations shall worship before Him	Genesis 12:3; Psalm 22:27, 72:17; foreshadowed with Solomon: 1 Kings 8:41-43, 10:23-25; seen ahead by Isaiah 56:6-7	This outreach was initiated with Jesus: John10:16; Matthew 28:18-20; through His disciples the message has spread worldwide: Matthew 24:14; in the future there will be great diversity worshipping around the throne, seen here: Revelation 5:9-10, 14:6-7
King: descendant through David's line who will reign forever	2 Samuel 7:12-17; Psalm 2:6-7; Jeremiah 23:5; Micah 5:2	Matthew 1:1, 6, 2:6, 12:23, 21:9, 27:37, 28:18-20; John 18:37; Luke 1:32,33

NOT YET: what was predicted that is not yet realized

There are many visions of what Messiah will do that have clearly not occurred yet in human history. According to the visions given in the Bible these are what we can expect to see in a future time.

	FORSEEN	*NOT YET ACCOMPLISHED*
Revealing of world dictator	Daniel 7:8-10, 11:36-39; Matthew 24:15-21; Mark 13:14; 2 Thessalonians 2:3-4; Revelation 13:1-9	
Catastrophic world-wide disasters, and war	Daniel 11:40-45; Isaiah 28:22; Matthew 24:27-30; Luke 21:20-24; Revelation chapters 6-18	
Judah's brothers shall cry out, and bow down to Shiloh	Genesis 49:8; Isaiah 64:1-12; Zechariah 12:10-14	

	FORSEEN	*NOT YET ACCOMPLISHED*
A re-gathering and outpouring of His spirit on all sons of Israel	Jeremiah 31:31-37; Ezekiel 37:12-14,19-28; 39:27-29; Zechariah 12:1-14	
Messiah's arrival to accomplish great battle	Isaiah 34:1-8; Habakkuk 3:3-15; Micah 4:10-13; Zephaniah 1:15-18; Zechariah 9:14-17, 12:2-3,9, 14:1-4; Malachi 3:2, 4:2-3; Matthew 24:27-31; Acts 1:11; Revelation 17:12-14, 19:11-17	
Great destruction by fire	Micah 1:4; Isaiah 29:6, 66:16; Zephaniah 3:8; Malachi 4:1; 2 Peter 3:10-11	

	FORSEEN	*NOT YET ACCOMPLISHED*
Resurrection and immortality of all people: indicated by stages	Psalm 73:24-27; Job 19:23-27; Isaiah 26:19-21; Daniel 12:1-3; Ezekiel 37:12-14; John 5:25-29; 1 Corinthians 15:51-54; 1 Thessalonians 4:14-17; Revelation 20:4-6, then 11-14	
Judgment from Christ: also indicated by stages	Psalm 96:13; Ezekiel 20:33-38; Malachi 3:5-6; Matthew 25:31-46; Romans 14:10-12; Revelation 18:1-24, 19:17-21, 20:1-5,11-15	

	FORSEEN	*NOT YET ACCOMPLISHED*
Messianic Kingdom established on earth	Isaiah 2:2-3, 11:4-9; Jeremiah 31:38-40; Micah 4:1-4, 5:4-5; Zephaniah 3:9-15; Zechariah 8:3-8; Malachi 3:11-12; Revelation 20:5-6	
New Heavens and Earth	Isaiah 65:17-25, 66:18-24; Hebrews 11:10-16, 12:22; 2Peter 3:13; Revelation 21:1-2	

Acknowledgements

Every book has an acknowledgements page because any book is work, and no one brings anything to print alone. I say this as if it's a new idea because I've discovered it for myself.

I'm grateful to my husband Larry, who believed in and supported this project since it was first conceived. I am eternally thankful for the steady love from his blue eyes.

I will never forget Julie. Her words ignited my whole journey. I think of my best friend from high school, Toots, whose faith surprised me before I even cared. I am grateful to Anne, my friend from college who courageously brought her brand new Bible into my room and read to me from it. I am indebted to Dorothy Stromberg, an odd church lady, who came over to my house and showed me, as my babies napped, how to live off and be sustained by the words found in my own Bible.

Linda Dillow encouraged me to start writing. Then both Jenn Daniel and Barb Gemar urged me to keep going. The wordsmith Steven James gave me honest aesthetic critique. Pam Johnson, his editor and now my friend, spent hours cleaning up my word mess, and was willing to accept artwork for her effort. Thanks also to Eva Everson, Ben Wolf, Beth Jusino and Gwen

Diaz who helped me to adapt and refine this piece for you.

Susan Hooks's interest in the project gave access to some of the artists she represented at White Stone Gallery in Philadelphia. I am grateful to Aaron Gosser, Diane Hirt, Sandra Bowden, Carol Bomer, Kareem Blake and Barbara Februar for letting me excerpt their evocative work in this book. OJ and Myoshi Gardner's generosity at Buladeen Barn gave me space where I could focus on completing this project. Jody Dillow's theological critique helped my mystical artistic thinking stay gripped to the plow handle.

And firstly as well as lastly I acknowledge the Master Wordsmith, the Greatest Storyteller, the Author and the Finisher who is my Maker, who invites others like me into creative work, and then rests me in the assurance that this, even this, was appointed.

Artwork

About the Author

Mary Nees has been reading through and speaking up about the Bible in public and private settings for over 40 years. Her passion is to take major themes in biblical stories and distill them in ways that motivate people to begin seeing the story's relevance for their own lives.

Mary is a visual artist who trained at Cornell University and the Pennsylvania Academy of the Fine Arts. She holds a Master of Fine Arts degree from East Tennessee State University where she served as an adjunct faculty member. She has won various regional and some national awards for her artwork which can be viewed on her website www.marynees.com.

Cairn University in Langhorne, PA invited Mary to display 12 large monotypes on their campus for the 2012 school year. Mary is an active member in the professional organization CIVA, Christians in the Visual Arts.

In 2007, Mary presented a lecture at the University of Virginia, Wise Campus, on the subject of symbolism that speaks to culture. She has also lectured and conducted workshops at the prestigious Luxun Academy of Fine Arts as well as at Shenyang University, and Qingdao University in the People's Republic of China.

Mary met her husband Larry in college

where both of them were exploring the reliability of the Bible and the real identity of Jesus. Now they invest time together training younger Christian leaders overseas. They have four grown kids and six precious grandchildren.

Notes

[1] You would do well to check this out for yourself rather than taking my word for it. But here's a taste: from Confucius' *Analects,* the original Buddha's quest for nirvana, Muhammad's recounting of the visions from the angel, to the book of Mormon (and lots of similar in between guides) you will find steps and recommendations for how one can make it to peace or find a way to God. In my view, all of this is self-help. The reader is left to trust the vision of some man, one who himself needs help. In none of these writings is there sound assurance from God Himself as the way to be safe. The Bible is significantly different.

[2] Few of what are considered the great religious works in literature make any claim to be words actually communicated by the God of all gods. Eastern works, like Hinduism's *Rig Veda*, and *Upanishads*; Buddhism's *Pali Canon*; or the Tibetan *Book of the Dead* indicate the Eastern view that God is not a person who speaks, but rather a force removed. Confucius' Analects were venerable principles for social order, but Confucius himself, though he accepted the idea of an Originator never claimed to have heard from Him. The Koran is considered by Muslims as the words of God (only in Arabic) those words having been transmitted by an angel; Allah Himself is portrayed in the Koran however as impossible to grasp, unknowable, not predictable nor rational. The concept of the Creator Himself, entering into many human histories, speaking directly, predicting the future is entirely

unique in the Hebrew and Greek biblical texts compared with any other religious documents.

INTRODUCTION

[3] As qtd. in L'Engle, Madeleine, *And It Was Good: Reflections on Beginnings.* Shaw Books, 1983. p.181.

[4] Excerpted from the first stanza of Yeats' poem, "The Second Coming" 1921.

MARKER 1

[5] First lines in Yeats' poem "The Second Coming" 1921. Last Accessed January 21, 2015. *http://www.poetryfoundation.org/poem/172062*

[6] Genesis 1:29-30; 2:9,16-17 All manner of good fruit was created, planted and given to man to "eat freely," but one tree was specifically warned against: "the tree of the knowledge of good and evil." Genesis 2:17 (note all references throughout are from the New American Standard Bible, NASB, unless otherwise noted).

[7] Genesis 3:20 "Now the man called his wife's name Eve, because she was the mother of all the living."

[8] Genesis 4:1

[9] Genesis 2-3, particularly 3:8

[10] Genesis 4:25; Leviticus 17:11; 2 Chronicles 36:23; Ezra 1:12; Acts 10:42, 22:14; 1 Corinthians 12:28

[11] Psalm 113:5-6

[12] Psalm 113:6, ESV

[13] Genesis 3:9

[14] Matthew 7:14

[15] Amos 3:3

[16]Jesus agreed that there are few who walk with God, John 2:23-25, Matthew 8:10-12; yet He also kept looking for those few. Matthew 7:13-14, John 15:1-11.

MARKER 2

[17] As qtd. in Rothstein, Muschamp and Marty, *Visions of Utopia*. Oxford University Press, 2003. p.14.

[18] Genesis 4:26

[19] Genesis 4:26

[20] Exodus 33:11a NIV

[21] Exodus 3:2

[22] Exodus 3:4

[23] Exodus 2:11-15

[24] Psalm 90:4, 12

[25] Both of Jesus' parents were described as faithful, spiritually responsive Jews. Mary was said to have "found favor with God" Luke 1:30. Matthew's account highlights Joseph as a "righteous man" 1:19. Faithful Hebrews would have taken seriously the command from Deuteronomy to speak, honor and teach of God in

every opportunity of daily life, Deuteronomy 6:1-9, specifically for the purpose of passing on their knowledge, fear and love of God to their offspring.

[26] Luke 2:41-52

[27] Isaiah 63:16

[28] Luke 2:52 ERV

[29] Matthew 6:1

[30] Matthew 6:5

MARKER 3

[31] Matthew 7:7-8

[32] Matthew 7:11 MSG

[33] Luke 11:1-8

[34] Psalm 116:1

[35] Genesis 4:26

[36] Auden, W.H. Van Gogh: *A Self Portrait; Letters Revealing His Life as a Painter.* E.P. Dutton and Co., 1963. p. 55, Letter of July 1880

[37] Pascal, Blaise. *Pascal's Pensees.* E.P. Dutton, 1958. p.121.

[38] Genesis 3:16

[39] Exodus through Deuteronomy

[40] Enoch is introduced, and marked out as one who "walked with God" Genesis 5:22.

[41] The 2nd law of thermodynamics: Last Accessed

January 21, 2015.
http://www.emc.maricopa.edu/faculty/farabee/bi obk/biobookener1.html

[42] Genesis 4:23-24

[43] Genesis 5:22-24

[44] What's even more interesting is that the original Hebrew puts a definite article before the word that we translate as *God* to emphasize that "Enoch walked with *the* God." The language insertion here in the text is to make sure you don't miss it. This is not just any god—this is *the* God (as opposed to any trumped up alternative by this time in human history). Enoch is walking with "the Real Deal."

[45] Genesis 4:26

[46] Genesis 5:22-25

[47] Genesis 6:9

[48] Exodus 24:4

[49] Genesis 6:5-7 NIV

[50] He always does, as He said later to one prophet: Amos 3:7: "Surely the Lord does nothing unless He reveals His secret counsel to His servants the prophets."

[51] Genesis 20:11

[52] Genesis 15:1

[53] Genesis 20:17

[54] Proverbs 1:7 and in many places following that

introduction, Solomon discourses on this important concept.

[55] The word can also mean loveliness or beauty. The Hebrew root of this word gives the idea of a superior being bending low in kindness before an inferior. Noah, the inferior in this case, has something given to him: grace or favor.

[56] Genesis 6:8 Last Accessed January 21, 2015. *http://biblehub.com/genesis/6-8.htm*

[57] Exodus 33:20

[58] Matthew 5:20

[59] Matthew 15:11

[60] Matthew 6:22-23

[61] Matthew 5:6

[62] Deuteronomy 33:16

[63] Genesis 6:5

MARKER 4

[64] Stated in 1958-59, as qtd. in *Art Forum*, December 2010. p.191.

[65] Prominent Galleries in NYC and London have had shows recently titled "Abstraction of Destruction," and "Those Who Remain," My local University decided to join the fray with a juried show in 2012 called "The Day on Fire."

[66] God laid out the standard, speaking to Moses, that any one claiming to be a prophet would need to be 100% accurate, or otherwise disregarded.

"The Bible lays out its claim for inspiration in such a way that it can be either substantiated or disproved." Last Accessed October 28, 2015.

http://y-jesus.com/wwrj/5-was-jesus-messiah/4/. Not only does God claim the authority of His words given in the Bible, He said in Deuteronomy 18 that anyone claiming to be a prophet needed to be scrutinized for complete accuracy.

[67] Walvoord, John. *The Prophecy Knowledge Handbook,* SP Publications Inc., 1990. p.10.

[68] You will not find such distinct and exact claims about future events in any other religious texts. The comparison is actually stunning if you'll take time to check this out for yourself. The Bible stands alone for its specific detail on our beginning as a created race and much more detail about our end.

[69] 2 Kings 5:10

[70] 2 Kings 20:1-11; 2 Chronicles 32:24-33; Isaiah 38

[71] Genesis 2:17 NIV (emphasis added)

[72] Walvoord, John. *The Prophecy Knowledge Handbook.* p.20.

[73] Genesis 3:9 (emphasis added)

[74] In two of my English translations the sentences indent the next section reflecting this change that is seen in the original textual formatting. Hebrew scholars have told me that this is very evident in the original language. This is a fascinating literary

device that God is using.

[75] Genesis 3:15

[76] The serpent will be "bruised" on the head. The word used here can be translated "to snap," "to break," or "to overwhelm," while the woman's seed will be bruised on the heel, a sign of fight. The hope given here is shrouded in battle words. But it's certain because God says it, and that's all that He says about it.

[77] Genesis 2:17, then 3:15

[78] see Appendix

[79] Habakkuk 2:4

[80] For a short but poignant example of this, read the 3 chapters of Habakkuk's vision.

[81] How about other trail maps, other prophetic claims outside the Bible? Be alert, as God says through Moses, to test prophets for the veracity of their detail in time. One inaccurate and disproven claim means a complete fail. According to God's test for authenticity, anyone claiming to be a prophet from God carries a responsibility for precise accuracy. Listeners need to listen carefully, and disregard anyone prophesying who makes even one false claim. To claim to speak for God is serious business. Deuteronomy 18:20

[82] For each true prophet, the events he spoke of that were soon fulfilled in his present time were necessary and validated his authority to speak about anything else in distant future. 100%

accuracy was the expectation for the job.
Deuteronomy 18:20-22

[83] Last Accessed October 28, 2015.
https://bible.org/book/export/html/6458

[84] Habakkuk 3:2

[85] Habakkuk 3:3-15

[86] Habakkuk 3:16

[87] Habakkuk 3:17-19

MARKER 5

[88] Dickens, Charles. *A Tale of Two Cities*. Book 1,
Chapter 5.

[89] Genesis 3:15

[90] Matthew 3:2

[91] John 1:29

[92] John 1:31 and 33

[93] Matthew 11:3

[94] Isaiah 35:5

[95] Isaiah 61:1

[96] Matthew 11:4-6

[97] Matthew 13:55; Mark 6:3

[98] Isaiah 61:1-2a

[99] Luke 4:21

[100] Luke 4:14-30

[101] Matthew 13:55

[102] The collection of 66 chapters in Isaiah's long work interestingly mirrors the Bible's entire collection of 66 books and is divided exactly the same way between a 1st collection of 39 units and a 2nd collection of 27 units. Isaiah's chapters 1-39 are primarily warnings of judgment. Chapter 40 initiates a significant change in Isaiah's tone with the following chapters 40-66 giving many promises of hope. This mirrors the tone of the Old Testament, which is 39 books, contrasting with the 27 books in the New Testament that reveal God's hope.

[103] Last Accessed January 21, 2015. *http://server.firefighters.org/stedman/stedmanlibrary/stedman/adventure/0223.html*

[104] Matthew 4:17

[105] Matthew 5:17

[106] Isaiah 61:2b

[107] Deuteronomy 18:15-22

[108] See Mark 2:1-2 for one story where a broad prophetic claim was then validated by an immediate present tense event.

[109] John 3:17, 12:47

[110] Luke 19:10; Matthew 18:11; John 3:17 and 12:47

[111] Isaiah 61:2b

[112] First coined by Oscar Cullmann, "already/not

yet" aptly describes the language for time used in both the Hebrew and Greek scriptures. It is a summary statement that resolves the progressive already-established plan of redemptive history through the march of time. The present "now," or "today," is always the point of urgent call in faith relative to what has already occurred and also what is still yet to be fully completed. For a detailed discussion of this see Cullmann's *Christ and Time; The Primitive Christian Conception of Time and History*. Trans. Floyd V. Filson. The Westminster Press, 1964, p.86. For a simple summary, see my Appendix

[113] See Appendix

[114] Genesis 3:7, 21

[115] Psalm 22:16-18; Isaiah 50:6, 53:1-12; Daniel 9:24-26; Zechariah 12:10; Hosea 5:15-6:3

[116] John 3:17-19

[117] John 4:26

[118] John 8:24-29, 58

[119] Isaiah 53; Luke 24:25-32

[120] John 14:6

[121] John 3:17, John 12:27

[122] Matthew 9:30, 12:16-21, 17:9-12; Mark 1:44, 3:12, 5:43, 7:36-27, 9:9; Luke 4:41-44, 9:20-22

123 John 5:22, 27; Matthew 25:31-46

[124] A summary of difficult days to come, according

to the Prophets, is available on request by contacting the author: *www.marynees.com*

[125] Matthew 24:21

[126] Matthew chapters 24 through 25

[127] John 10:7-9

MARKER 6

[128] Elliot, Elisabeth. *The Bible's Light for Your Daily Walk.* Revell, 2013. Day 11.

[129] Bonhoeffer, Dietrich. *Letters and Papers from Prison.* Fortress Press, 2010. Letter of January 29-30, 1944.

[130] Hebrews 2:1-3

[131] John 1:1

[132] John 10:14-28

[133] Revelation 1:1

[134] Revelation 1:17-18

[135] Isaiah 21:2-3; Jeremiah 20:9; Daniel 8:27; 10:7-8; Revelation 1:17

[136] Hollander, Jean. "Switzerland; The Eighth Day After Creation." Last Accessed January 21, 2015. *http://imagejournal.org/page/journal/articles/issue-71/hollander-poem*

[137] Lewis, C.S. "The Lion, The Witch and the Wardrobe." *The Complete Chronicles of Narnia.* Harper Collins, 1998. p.99.

[138] Revelation 19:11

[139] Romans 10:17

[140] Hosea 5:11-15

[141] Mark 10:17-22

[142] Mark 10:27

[143] John 20:25

[144] John 20:26-31

[145] Revelation 1:18

[146] Lewis, C.S. *Mere Christianity*; Revised and enlarged edition. Harper, 2001. p.176.

[147] As qtd. in Pippert, R.M. *Hope Has Its Reasons; the Search to Satisfy Our Deepest Longings*. Revised edition. IVP Books, 2001. p.105.

MARKER 7

[148] Dillard, Annie. *The Writing Life*. Harper & Row, Publishers, 1989. p.73.

[149] Hebrews 2:15

[150] *http://thinkexist.com/quotation/nobody-gets-out-of-here/1515899.html*

[151]

http://www.azlyrics.com/lyrics/peggylee/isthatallt hereis.html

[152] Genesis 16:8

[153] Genesis 16:13

[154] Genesis 21:17

[155] Genesis 3:23

[156] Genesis 3:22

[157] Steir, Pat as qtd. in Dazzling Water, Dazzling Light, interview by Barbara Weidle, Seattle: University of Washington Press, 2000. p.75.

[158] Hebrews 11:10

[159] Job 1:1

[160] Job 19:23-25

[161] Deuteronomy 34: 1-4

[162] Psalm 22:26

[163] Psalm 29:10

[164] Psalm 41:12 ISV

[165] Psalm 68:21-22

[166] Habakkuk 3:3-15

[167] Malachi 4:1-2

[168] See Micah 5:2-5; Zephaniah 3:9-20, Compare Isaiah 11:1-5 with Revelation 5:5-10, and 22:16. See also 2 Peter 3:9-13, and Revelation 21:1-7

[169] John 14:1-7 TLB

[170] Luke 23:42-43

[171] John 3:15, 4:14, 5:24, 6:40, 7:38, 8:24, 9:39, 10:28, 11:25, 12:25, 13:20, 14:23, 15:11, 16:16, 17:2, 24, 18:36, 19:30, 20:29, 21:19

[172] 1 Peter 1:3-5 MSG

[173] Revelation 1:3

[174] John 12:48 Listen to Jesus' warnings: Matthew 7:13-27, Luke 16:19-31, John 5:24, also John 3:16-18 (speaking to a respected religious man) "For God so loved the world, that He gave His only begotten Son, that whoever believes in Him should not perish, but have eternal life. For God did not send the Son into the world to judge the world, but that the world should be saved through him. He that believes in him is not judged; he who does not believe has been judged already, because he has not believed in the name of the only begotten Son of God."

[175] Accessed January 21, 2015. *http://peacewithgod.net/that-whoever-believes-in-him/?*

[176] John 10:16

EPILOGUE

[177] Here's a free and reliable site for Bible reading: *https://www.biblegateway.com*

[178] Hebrews 4:12; 2 Timothy 3:16

APPENDIX

[179] Pentecost, Dwight. *Things to Come*. Dunham Publishing, 1958. pp.245-246

Made in the USA
Coppell, TX
21 February 2021

50629518R00105